EXPLORING THE MATRIX

Visions of the Cyber Present

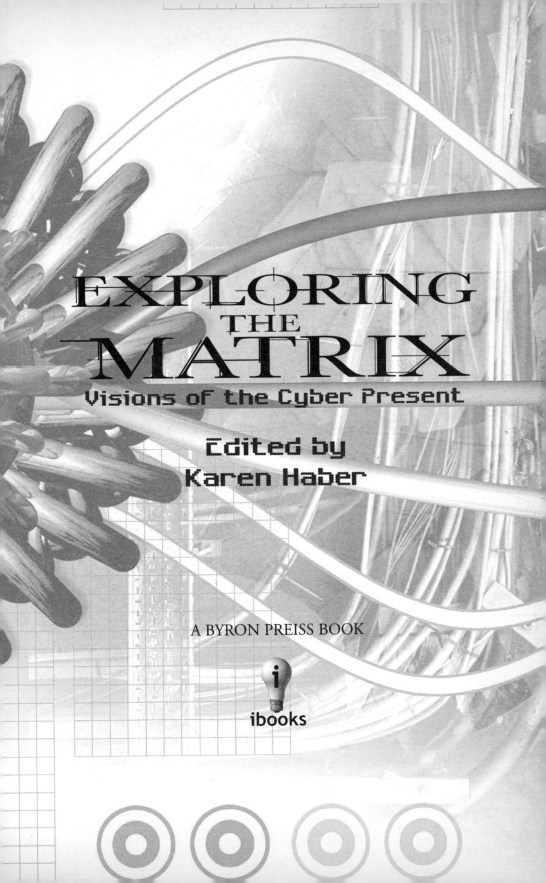

EXPLORING
THE
MATRIX

Visions of the Cyber Present

Edited by
Karen Haber

A BYRON PREISS BOOK

ibooks

Editor: Karen Haber
Project Editor: Howard Zimmerman
Designed by J. Vita
Interior illustrations, pages 5, 30–31 (and inserts), 74–75 (and inserts), 98–99 (and inserts), 112–113 (and inserts), 122–123 (and inserts), 148–149 (and inserts), 180–181 (and inserts), 200–201 (and inserts), 250–251 (and inserts) copyright © 2003 Darrel Anderson
Interior iullustrations, pages 2–3, 6–7, 8, 9, 16–17 (and inserts), 48–49 (and inserts), 64–65 (and inserts), 136–137 (and inserts), 168–169 (and inserts), 212–213 (and inserts), 222–223 (and inserts), 236–237 (and inserts) copyright © 2003 Robert Zohrab
Jacket illustration copyright © 2003 Robert Zohrab

Introduction copyright © 2003 Karen Haber.
"Every Other Movie Is the Blue Pill" copyright © 2003 Bruce Sterling
"The Real Matrix" copyright © 2003 Stephen Baxter
"The Matrix: Know Thyself" copyright © 2003 John Shirley
"Art Imitates Life (Yes, It's News)" copyright © 2003 Darrel Anderson
"Literary Influences on The Matrix" copyright © 2003 Paul Di Filippo
"More Than You'll Ever Know: Down The Rabbit Hole of The Matrix" copyright © 2003 Kathleen Ann Goonan
"The Matrix and the Star Maker" copyright © 2003 Mike Resnick
"Yuen Woo-þing and the Art of Flying" copyright © 2003 Walter Jon Williams
"Alice in Metropolis or It's All Done with Mirrors" copyright © 2003 Dean Motter
"The Matrix as Simulacrum" copyright © 2003 Ian Watson
"The Matrix as Sci-Fi" copyright © 2003 Joe Haldeman
"Tomorrow May Be Different" copyright © 2003 David Brin
"Revenge of the Nerds, Part X" copyright © 2003 Alan Dean Foster
"Reflection in a Cyber Eye" copyright © 2003 Karen Haber
"Meditations on the Singular Matrix" copyright © 2003 James Patrick Kelly
"The Matrix Made Me Do It" copyright © 2003 Kevin J. Anderson
"Dreaming Real" copyright © 2003 Rick Berry

Distributed by Simon & Schuster U.K. Ltd

www.simonsays.co.uk

ISBN 0-7434-7502-X

3 5 7 9 10 8 6 4 2

For Mike Benko—
He knows why

CONTENTS

INTRODUCTION

What Is The Matrix . . . and Why Is It Such a Big Deal?

Pat Cadigan

The question I hear most often in interviews conducted by people with only a passing acquaintance with science fiction is, "What drew you to science fiction?" It's not always worded exactly that way, but that's the gist. It's not an easy question to answer. You're drawn to science fiction in much the same way you're drawn to a type of music—something in it speaks to you, bone-deep.

This makes it sound like something for a specialized audience with particular tastes, and there's a certain degree of truth to that. Those who like the stuff follow their favorite writers, or TV series, or, yes, movies with a devotion that, say, Red Sox fans would find familiar. And much in the same way that certain professional athletes attract the kind of notice that takes them beyond prominence in their sports to full celebrity status, certain things that originate squarely in the science fiction world—or universe—break out and attract a following beyond genre aficionados. *Star Trek* is probably the most famous example of a breakout hit; *Star Wars* is another. And the most recent is *The Matrix*.

Oddly enough, the breakout media blockbuster is more often than not science fiction, or a close relative (e.g., *Buffy the Vampire Slayer*). Oddly, because science fiction itself is more often than not treated like a punchline by everyone from critics and commentators to the bookstores' best customers. Oprah's Book Club didn't last long enough for anyone to start second-guessing what kind of books might be favored but I think it's safe to say that even if it had outlived Oprah herself by a hundred years, chances are slim to none that a science fiction novel would have gotten the nod even once.

If that isn't odd enough for you, consider this: Universities around the world offer Masters degree programs in science fiction and have done so for something like thirty years—post *Star Trek* and pre *Star Wars*.

In short, science fiction is: 1) an area of extreme commercial success; 2) a hotbed of advanced intellectual discourse; and 3) too trivial to deserve the notice or attention of serious cultural commentators and critics. Only human nature itself would seem to embody as many contradictions. Personally, I don't think this is a coincidence.

The genre of the fantastic, which comprises science fiction, fantasy, horror, and all the shadings and gradations in between, is a clear and unmistakable indication of sentience. Why? Because only sentient creatures are capable of conceiving of something outside the realm of known experience; only the sentient are capable of living beyond their physical senses. If the nature of life itself is yes or no, alive or dead—binary, if you will—then the nature of conscious life is true or false, which is completely different. If, as the saying goes, Man is the animal who laughs, Man is also the animal who lies—i.e., makes up stories. From the very beginning, these stories were long on fantastic elements—gods, goddesses, monsters, demons, angels, and miracles, not to mention the occasional and/or imminent apocalypse. These are the elements human beings have used to build their legends. That we're still doing so today is quite significant, I'd say.

For one thing, it proves conclusively and without a doubt that the whole storytelling thing that started all those millennia ago wasn't just a trend after all. Think about it—even the whole hunter-gatherer thing was just a phase.

Actually, if any marriage was made in heaven, it's that of the movies with science fiction. Especially now—our dreams, fantasies, nightmares, and mythologies can be externalized like never before and the technology improves by Superman-style leaps and bounds. So it's hardly any mystery as to why we want to think about, talk about, argue about, analyse, theorize, and decode what we watch on the silver screen, and then watch some more. Since science fiction at its best is the literature of ideas, enormous amounts of creativity, art, and science go into the creation of those ideas as well as finding ways to give them external form. The effects from these things are quite far-reaching. I mean, as worthwhile and important as films like *American Beauty* and *The Usual Suspects* are, they wouldn't demand the creation of, say, Industrial Light & Magic or Skywalker Studios—though they certainly do see some benefits after the fact.

Of course, not all science-fiction movies are significant works of high intellectual art any more than all movies in general are created equal to *American Beauty* or *The Usual Suspects*. Nor does the fact that a movie is science fiction automatically make it a finer, greater creation than any other. And vice versa—which is to say, a movie is not pop culture junk food simply because it's science fiction to begin with.

And this final caveat, which I feel has too often gone unmentioned: If it's both science fiction and a significant work of high intellectual art, it's still science fiction. Got that?

Many of us in the field have watched people in the so-called mainstream produce work that is plainly and unmistakably science fiction and then claim emphatically that the work in question isn't science fiction at all. Sometimes they'll call it a "near-future thriller" or "a myth retold in a contemporary setting" or (my favorite) "boldly original and imaginative." And yeah, it probably is—and it's science fiction. We wouldn't mind, except that so many of these people who think they are, uh, going where no one has gone before (to phrase a coin) are just reinventing the wheel, and doing it badly.

We professionals are a tough audience, we are. Only one audience is tougher: *our* audience. So you may take the fact that *The Matrix* can inspire an entire book's worth of essays from experienced professionals in the field as high praise indeed.

All right, you're saying to yourself, so what *is* the big deal about *The Matrix*?

The essays that follow will cover that, in much glorious and contradictory detail. Traditions will be surveyed, lineages traced, perspectives laid out, challenged, defended, rearranged in ways that will have you conducting mental conversations and arguments with the authors. And a distinguished bunch they are, too. While none of them is quite old enough to have *invented* this particular wheel (no, not even you, Resnick), they've all had an effect on its function and design to some degree. A few, like John Shirley and Bruce Sterling, were among the vanguard that took it to the level where *The Matrix* could come into being in the first place. Others like Steve Baxter and Kathleen Ann Goonan demonstrate that there's no limit to the new spins you can put on it. Pretty impressive, the lot of them; just wait till you see what they do with your mind.

It's that aforementioned hotbed of intellectual discourse, and all to do with something that also happens to be an extreme commercial success. Now, the generally accepted folk-wisdom on these matters states that anything with some intelligence in it cannot possibly be commercial while any commercial success won't have enough intelligent substance to fill a shot glass. It's always been satisfying to see that sweeping generalization bite the dust, though I have to confess that I haven't been enjoying it as much as I used to. I've seen it happen often enough over the course of one lifetime that I'm starting to get a little impatient. I'd have thought that of all the lessons human beings had to learn, this would be one of the easier ones.

Like I said earlier, even the whole hunter-gatherer thing was just a phase.

Every Other Movie Is the Blue Pill

Bruce Sterling

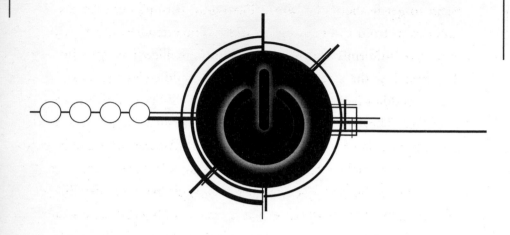

To make *The Matrix* cost over sixty million dollars. I don't know if you've ever hung out much with people commanding dozens of millions of dollars. Once I attended the World Economic Forum, where the planet's ultra-rich people flock in large crowds. This event took place in New York, in the jittery, heavily armed post-9/11 period, and the vibe there was very, very *Matrix* indeed.

There were swarms of armed bodyguards, marbled halls with swishing bronze elevators, glum, impassive federal agents, expensive eyewear, Forum groupies in sexy tailored costumes, the Secret Service in black bulletproof SWAT gear. . . . Very intense, very out-there, very designery, very Wachowski Brothers.

The World Economic Forum is not supposed to be scary. It's a philanthropic event. The Forum is all for the public good, and the worldwide betterment of the human condition. That is the public rationale, at least. That is the Blue Pill version, as it were.

However, you don't have to be a Seattle rioter or Naomi Klein to get it about the World Economic Forum's extreme disconnection from the man-in-the-street. The attendees there . . . they were uniformly courteous and scarily intelligent people, but they bear just the same relationship to a middle-class American that a middle-class American bears to an illiterate Venezuelan *campesino*. They are from a different level of reality. They dwell in a seamless world of private jets to the WaldorfAstoria, where public space is the eight feet between the doorman and the limo.

Much the same goes for the galactic gulf that separates *The Matrix* from its street-level inspirations in underground comix and sci-fi paperbacks. I doubt that anyone understands this better than Larry and Andy Wachowski. Somehow, and I give them every credit, they were able to metabolize the Hollywood red pill and leap to the dizziest levels of the military-entertainment complex. I've never met the Wachowski Brothers, but I have every confidence that they get it. Otherwise, two guys with their exquisite design sense would never choose to wear Converse sneakers and backwards baseball caps.

Luc Besson directed the science-fiction film *The Fifth Element*, a film that eats at the same cafeteria with *The Matrix*, feasting at a global gumbo of counterculture sources. Luc Besson was at the World Economic Forum sitting at a table behind me, and he was the worst-dressed guy in the WaldorfAstoria. Luc was so bad-boy, so confrontational, so in-your-face, that it was indescribable in any language other than French. And Luc really belonged there, that was the good part. When those Swiss captains of industry saw Luc in his four-day beard and bulging monocolor T-shirt, it cheered them all up. They sort of glanced at him sidelong and whispered. They were honored, really.

The Matrix may have budgeted for sixty-eight million, but for an ailing Warner Bros. it brought in way over two hundred million, and that was before the sequels. That was before the plastic action figures, the animé cartoons, comic books and the thriving online *Matrix* cult groups. I enjoyed the hell out of that movie, and five years later I was still thinking about it fondly, and finally getting around to making this arch critical assessment. Man, a record like that speaks for itself.

Contemporary movie people, especially supremely rich and powerful ones like Steven Spielberg, they really get it about the homely authenticity of Levi's jeans and white tube-socks. Because they know all about how to dress very attractive people very attractively. They've got it down to a literal science, they can measure the colored glint off polyvinyl with digital light meters. Why would movie pros ever dress like their actors? If you're a director and you dress up like a star, it's like confessing to your colleagues that you swallowed the baited hook.

Therefore, in *The Matrix*'s "real world," that world where giant Geof Darrow drawings writhe their tentacles and harvest babies like cantaloupes, all the *Matrix* heroes, slinky Trinity, delphic Morpheus, they have to wear collarless, ragged, functional clothes. They eat oatmeal and work overtime. Just like the Wachowskis do.

Whenever they leap through a telephone into the Matrix, however, they instantly become rich glamour people. They've got limos, couture clothes, and fully booked agendas. They've got bodyguards—actually, they are their own bodyguards, because they're also comic-book superheroes.

Their furniture shows up out of nothingness, as if they'd Web-clicked it off Design Within Reach. They have an infinite number of guns . . . an elite education comes in a plug-in cartridge . . . they are regal, kinky aristocrats.

What little we learn about these people in the early part of the film suggests that they are fanatical terrorists. Morpheus is an international fugitive. Trinity is a crooked hacker who broke an IRS code. But they're not outlaws, not really.

Because they never have to rob, swindle, corrupt, bribe or steal. They don't take drugs, have psychotic episodes, or do jail time, the homely, everyday things that most actual criminals do routinely.

They're not criminals, hackers or terrorists. They're masters of illusion. So if the *Matrix* people have a functional equivalent in contemporary society, it's not the Cosa Nostra or the Baader-Meinhof gang. It's Hollywood producers. Because they possess enormous resources, all out proportion to the flimsy nature of their enterprise. They can create and deflate vast fantasies at will. And yet, their lives and careers are in constant danger. Just like Warner Bros. executives!

As Howard Waldrop once said, all science fiction is really about science fiction. Movies tend to be really about movies. Movies are what movie people find most interesting in life. For real movie people, even bad movies are magic. Any act of cinema is magic for movie people, just like movies were magic when Méliès, the French stage magician, was inventing them.

Let's consider the justly famous dojo sequence in *The Matrix*. A dojo is not a place where people really fight. A dojo is a stage; it's a place to train and mimic fighting. In this scene,

Morpheus is teaching Neo how to fight. But what he is really teaching Neo is how to think about the art of violence. And the real freight being hauled here is two young, breakout American filmmakers teaching Hollywood how to film action sequences.

You see, you don't need Hollywood stunt doubles! Not at all! That's just habit! Instead, you hire top-flight kung-fu action people from distant, global-economy Hong Kong, to fully train the actors so that they can act while they're fighting!

And now, check out this "bullet-time" part where we *freeze stuff* just like a Marvel Comics two-page center spread! Watch and learn: now we *wheel around it* with this elaborate circle of synchronized cameras. See what we just did there? You think that was *air* we were breathing? Stop *trying* to make action films and *make* one!

The Wachowski Brothers are too young to be real cyberpunks. Besides, they work in the wrong industry. The do however have one great commonality with cyberpunk science fiction. They can't resist opening up the fabric of their artwork to stuff in every single idea they have ever had in their entire lives. In cyberpunk critical diction, this practice is known as "eyeball kicks." This term was first coined for the graphically overloaded comics pages of *MAD* magazine, so it is a cultural contribution of comics to science fiction. *Blade Runner* had it. *The Matrix* has it in spades.

H. G. Wells declared there should be only one weird element in every scientific romance. Wells was an author in a solemn Edwardian world that would allow itself only one or two really weird elements. Any more than that, and you weren't entertaining anymore; instead, you were raving and blaspheming.

The Wachowskis are native sons of the 1990s. It is impossible for them to think in such a limited way. If they ever found a world with just one freaky thing going on, they would assume they were in a cemetery.

In *The Matrix*, everything is going on. It's been blenderized and synthesized. It's tossed like brain salad.

First and most importantly, the film's got pop appeal elements. *All* kinds of elements: suicidal attacks by elite special forces, crashing helicopters, oodles of martial arts, a chaste yet passionate story of predestined love, bug-eyed monsters of the absolute first water, fetish clothes, captivity and torture and daring rescue, plus really weird, cool submarines.

Some of my favorite films are made entirely of clichés: *Casablanca, Every Which Way but Loose, The Prisoner of Zenda*. They're clichés, yes, but they have broken free of that problem, because the clichés slide through the narrative at refreshing orthogonal angles. In *Casablanca* the clichés are always tipping their hats at each other, "Hello war movie trope; pleased to meet you, women's weepy riff; how do you do, police procedural." They backflip from cliché to archetype. They generate tremendous narrative power. The clichés no longer tire us in these movies; they exhilarate.

The Matrix is a postmodern philosophical movie in which fragments of *philosophy* do this *Casablanca* cliché dance. There's Christian exegesis, a Redeemer myth, a death and rebirth, a hero in self-discovery, the Odyssey, Jean Baudrillard (lots of Baudrillard, the best parts of the film), science-fiction ontological riffs of the Philip K. Dick school, Nebuchadnezzar, the Buddha, Taoism, martial-arts mysticism, oracular prophecy, spoon-bending telekinesis, Houdini stage-show magic, Joseph Campbell, and

Godelian mathematical metaphysics.

This is a real mess. It would seem like a farrago if not for the film's premiere genius move, which is to reveal that the lysergic nightmare of cyborganic human-farms is this narrative's base reality. That's where people are born and die, and the rest of it is so much pixels. Since the world is a nightmare, the behavior of the bio-robot überlords makes no coherent sense. It isn't required to gel. If it ever gelled, it would lose its power. It would no longer be dreamlike, so it wouldn't tap in to the huge yet remarkably stupid creative powers of the Surrealist unconscious mind.

This brilliant concept allows every bit-part of metaphysics to float like flakes in a snow-globe, tight, contained, glittering, fragmented, and cheap. You get all the intellectually sexy head-trip

kicks of philosophizing without any of the boring hassles of consistency or rigor. It conveys the dark, goofy thrill of reading Milton or Dante when you're really stoned. I don't know how this wack stunt can ever be repeated, but that is one of the greatest achievements ever in the science-fiction cinema.

True, it veers perilously close to another Wells problem: "If anything is possible, nothing is interesting." But that's where the design comes in. In *The Matrix*, everything always and infallibly *looks* interesting. The visual tone is never lost; as moving images on a screen, the thing is as coherent as a laser.

Movie critics tend to wallow in the auteur theory: If anything cool happened, then Larry or Andy must have done it. But no one spends sixty-eight million dollars on the efforts of two people.

Geof Darrow must have come pretty cheap—all he needs is a pencil and paper—but he was the genius behind the writhing technorganic look of *The Matrix*'s version of hell. The high-concept guru guidance here came from Kevin Kelly, the magisterial author of *Out of Control: The New Biology of Machines, Social Systems, and the Economic World. Out of Control* is a Californian work of pop-science speculation that is one of my personal favorites. It is a very Petri dish of unwritten science-fiction novels.

Geof Darrow is an American midwesterner, like the Wachowskis, who hale from Chicago. Darrow threw that over to move to France and hang out with Moebius and the European *bande dessinée /Metal Hurlant* crowd. Geof Darrow is therefore a global comix artist.

It used to be that if you worked in a downmarket artform like comix, you were so dirt-poor that you didn't know much or see much, other than the subway route from Queens to the office.

Geof Darrow draws comics and does TV kids' cartoons, and yet he is an international man-of-mystery and a genuine design sophisticate. There's just no getting around it: He's really good.

You cross Darrow's pencil with Kevin Kelly's visonary intensity and out comes a hellish monsterscape. It is so far beyond the conceptual and technical limits of rubber-monster '50s sci-fi that it looks like a movie from another species.

If a SETI dish decoded a message from Betelgeuse, and we saw that our new friends were some Geof Darrow robo-octopi doing their buck-and-wing, everybody would just sort of nod. In six hours there would be talking heads on CNN: "Oh yes. Those are alien beings, all right. We always thought they'd look like that. Completely divorced from earthly standards."

These Darrow sets have a weird beauty, but the accomplishment doesn't end there. In *The Matrix*, when one returns from hell to the Earth, the Earth possesses weird beauty. The frenetic dot-com daily life in the 1990s looks frail and menaced and perishable, as indeed it turned out to be. "Normality" freezes at a blink. You can run it back and forth, chop it like videotape. It has pathos, *mono no aware*, like Japanese cherry blossoms.

The clothing is very beautiful in *The Matrix*, a feat I credit to costume designer Kym Barrett. Kym Barrett is Australian. Oz is not generally noted for its couture industry, and Ms. Barrett does not make and market clothes. She makes theatrical costumes. She did tremendous work in *Romeo + Juliet*, the bizarre adaptation where the Capulets and Montagues are rival Miami drug-mafia clans. But she hit a career high note in *The Matrix*. They aren't just professionally tailored costumes. They come from the heart. They somehow convey a young Australian woman's passionate, painfully distanced love for European and Hollywood glamour. Behind the menace of the oil-slick PVCs, the trench coats, and the guns is a bright little girl with her nose pressed firmly on the cold glass of a display window.

Punk fashion has always been protective armor. The spikes, the leather, the razors, the zippers, they are what you put on after flower-power has choked to death on its own vomit. It's Kevlar for the soft marshmallow core of youthful idealism. Cynicism after the hard knocks of life, real *weltschmerz*, no future, they don't look like that.

You can't be dead, because I love you. That is the emotional core of *The Matrix*, and that is not an adult statement. That is a statement that a six-year-old girl would say to a dead kitten. And yet the dead beloved rises at a kiss, walks, and then kicks everybody's ass. I'm sorry, but it just doesn't matter how silly that is. That is beyond rational discourse. Anyone who can resist that is emotionally defunct.

Whenever you've written off *The Matrix* as a hippie fairy-tale, it always hits you upside the head with high-concept. Or with genuine political radicalism, as when the film's treacherous villain sells out to become Ronald Reagan. In America, Rage Against the Machine was so much CD-product, but Rage were ultra-left-wing radicals genuinely enraged by the machine. They scared the daylights out of police in Mexico City. It's like going down to Toys 'R' Us and finding out that they're retailing toddler's backpacks full of shattered glass.

That's no real problem if you're a Wachowski, a guy who can hold three different continents and eight different philosophies in your head at the same time. But you know, a society whose artists can do such things has some profound inherent dif-ficulties. Such unmoored, slippery, moral relativism, combined with such glossy, with-it, magazine-spread prosperity, arouses some fierce resentments. If you are the kind of guy who can only manage one continent and one philosophy, then you want to hijack their aircraft and crash them into their skyscrapers. Not that this will improve their mood any. It's just that, well, it's very hard to dent them otherwise.

The same goes for rebels in *The Matrix*. If these are revolu-tionaries, then they have a hippie problem. The problem with hip-pie revolution is very simple: There's no victory condition. There's no strategy for change and no *novus ordo seclorum*. What happens if Neo wins? If everyone eats the Red Pill, there are billions of naked, atrophied wretches in big gooey pods fighting off flying killer robots with their bare hands. They have no jobs, no identities, no families, no laws, no civil order, no traditions, no hope, no ethics, no justice, no concept of what has happened to them. No nothing. They are meat on a ruined moonscape whose sky is falling and whose gods are mysterious, capricious, malign and all-powerful.

Small wonder that Neo runs back into the fantasy. He's living in the pixels, stepping out of a phone booth, and flying. That is his victory, limited and illusory though it is. The cyber-messiah didn't change a thing, not really; when it came to the crunch, it was all smoke and mirrors. But you know, at least he got his head around it. He went to the bottom of the rabbit hole. And that justly made him everybody's darling.

The Real Matrix

Stephen Baxter

There's something wrong with the world . . .
—Morpheus, *The Matrix*

Morpheus probably shares this insight with most of us, especially in our young teenage years. Generally we dismiss such feelings of out-of-jointedness as mere paranoia. In Neo's case following up that uneasiness actually led to the unravelling of reality as he had understood it.

Remarkably enough, however, there have been suggestions not only that simulated realities are a possibility of the future, but *that we may be living in one right now* [1, 2].

The scenario of the movie—the AI's with their bottle-bank humans used as power generators—may not be plausible. But if we *are* inside a simulation, who might be running it? Is there any way we could tell? Is there any way we could emulate Neo and break out?

And even if we could, should we?

Where are the aliens?

If they exist, we should see them. Because the likely time scales of the expansion of a civilization through the galaxy are so much shorter than the age of the galaxy itself, and given the evolution of at least one intelligent race (ourselves), we should have overwhelming evidence of the existence of others. But we don't.

Recent evidence for the existence of planets around other stars, and the accumulation of negative evidence for extraterrestrial intelligence after several decades of fruitless SETI programs, have only deepened the mystery. This is better known as the Fermi Paradox [3].

There are lots of possible answers, widely explored in science and science fiction. Perhaps there are "filters" that might destroy intelligences before they can make their presence known: atomic war, galactic core explosions. Then there are various "zoo hypotheses," conscious strategies that might cause other civilizations to conceal their presence from us—like *Star Trek*'s Prime Directive.

But the problem is consistency. You have to suppose that *every* species destroys itself, or is destroyed, or submits to a doctrine of concealment. It would take only one exception, one rogue Ferengi trader busting into the game reserve, for the quarantine to collapse. The Paradox is surely telling us that something is fundamentally wrong with our view of the universe and our place in it: There is something wrong with the world, indeed.

I have suggested that a plausible resolution of the Fermi Paradox is that *what we see around us is artificial* [1]. What if we have been placed in some form of "planetarium," perhaps generated using an advanced virtual reality technology, designed to give us the illusion of an empty universe—while beyond the walls with their painted stars, the shining lights of extraterrestrial civilizations glow unseen? This might seem outlandish, but it would resolve the

Paradox. And if you think about it, it's far easier to throw a cloak around one world, or even one solar system, than to mask an entire galactic culture. . . .

Or here's another possibility. What if the planetarium creators aren't aliens, but our own future descendants?

Nick Bostrom, a philosopher at Yale University, has suggested that we may all be living in a Matrix developed by a post-human society of the future [2] (though probably far beyond the 2199 timeframe of *The Matrix*). As we will see, there is certainly no theoretical limit to generating such a fake reality, though it is energy-hungry. We can't guess at the motives of the post-humans, any more than a Neandertal could guess at yours. But if it's possible to generate simulated universes with simulated consciousnesses inside, then it will surely be done; we humans tend to realize any possible technology.

Not only that, Bostrom chillingly argues that you are overwhelmingly *likely* to be living in such a simulation.

The argument goes like this. You may be living in the "original" version of history—but there's only one copy of that, while there are many more (infinitely many?) possible simulations of history. So, if you imagine your consciousness as a counter dropped at random into any one of the possible reality frames, it's a lot more likely you'd find yourself dropped into a sim than the real thing.

If, with our limited understanding, we can think of two plausible classes of simulation controllers, there are probably many more. Maybe we should indeed take the possibility seriously. But if we do, is there anything we can say about the properties of such a simulation?

There was of course speculation on artificial realities long before *The Matrix* itself, and its cyberpunk progenitors like William Gibson. We can trawl this material for clues about what kind of planetarium we might be living in. (A good recent review of modern thinking on the relation of reality to mind, computation and virtual reality is given by David Deutsch [4].)

The idea that the world around us may not be real reaches back to Plato, who wondered if what we see resembles the flickering shadows on a cave wall. The notion of creating deceptive artificial environments dates back at least as far as Descartes, who in the seventeenth century speculated on the philosophical implications of a sense-manipulating "demon"—effectively a pre-technological virtual-reality generator. A recent example is the movie *The Truman Show* (1999) in which the protagonist is the unwitting star of a TV show, trapped under a fake domed sky; early in the movie a spotlight crashes from sky to ground, bearing the label "Sirius."

In fake-reality science-fiction novels, the fake universe has sometimes turned out to be a generation starship, whose inhabitants are unaware that their world is merely the ship's interior. In Harry Harrison's *Captive Universe* [5] the crew's ignorance is engineered; harsh social engineering, taboos, rituals, and even genetic modification are used to keep the populace in their place. But in Brian Aldiss's *Non-Stop* [6] and Robert Heinlein's *Orphans of the Sky* [7] the crew have simply forgotten they are on a ship. Aldiss's dwarfed "dizzies" wander without comprehension through a hull crammed with vegetation, essentially driven insane by their endless confinement.

Alternatively, the artificial universes may be erected as

virtual-reality computer projections. This is an idea deployed in the TV series *Star Trek* with its holodecks, in which emulations of material objects are directly created around real humans. And of course in *The Matrix*, humans are forcibly immersed in a "neural-interactive simulation" via direct implants in their brains.

Possible planetariums have a variety of scopes, depending on how far the boundary of "reality" is set from the human consciousness. The crudest sort are like the one in *The Truman Show*, in which the people and the objects they touched were real, while the sky was a fake dome. Perhaps the stars and galaxies are simulated, along with artificial incoming starlight, by a great shell surrounding the solar system. Or perhaps *everything* beyond the atmosphere is a fake—or was, until humans reached the Moon. The engineering behind even a *Truman* planetarium would be impressive, though, as the builders would have to simulate not just photons but such exotica as cosmic rays and neutrinos. If they anticipate our technological progress, perhaps even now they are readying the gravity-wave generators. . . .

But the boundary of "reality" may be much closer to ourselves. Perhaps we humans are real, but, after the manner of *Star Trek*'s holodeck, some subset (or all) of the objects we see around us are generated as simulations, tangible enough to interact with our senses. Or perhaps even our bodies are simulated, as in *The Matrix*, so that the boundary of reality is close around our very consciousness.

The scope of the simulation will naturally impose different requirements on its builders; a **Truman** planetarium would presumably be much less energy-expensive to generate than a Matrix or holodeck. But a primary quality required of any such planetarium is, of course, its ability to fool inhabitants at least as smart as ourselves into believing that what they see is real.

Why do we believe that the universe is real in the first place? The most extreme contrary position, as set out by Bishop Berkeley, is the solipsistic notion that the apparently external world is contained within the observer's imagination. It might seem impossible to disprove this. After all, everything we experience is a virtual-reality rendering anyway, compiled by our unconscious minds from scraps of sensory data, plus theories, inborn and acquired, on how objects ought to behave.

Dr. Johnson gave a robust response to this [4]. When Boswell remarked on the impossibility of refuting Berkeley's theory, Johnson kicked a large rock and said, "I refute it *thus*." What Johnson meant was that when the rock "kicked back" at his foot, he either had to formulate a theory of physical law that explained the existence and behavior of the rock, or else assume that his imagination was itself a complex, autonomous universe *containing* laws that precisely simulated the existence of the rock—which would therefore be a more complex system. If the *simplest* explanation is that an object like Dr. Johnson's rock is autonomous, then we accept that that entity is real.

But we can turn Dr. Johnson's criterion around, and use it as a test of what is required of any simulation of the universe.

The universe must be *consistent*. We believe that in principle anybody anywhere could perform a scientific experiment of the finest detail on any sample of the universe and its contents, and should find the fabric of reality yielding consistent results. That is, the rocks must always "kick back" in the same way, no matter where and how we kick them.

Further, if the jailers wanted to fool their captives into believing there is no outside world, they would have to ensure that the environment was *self-contained*: that no explanations of anything inside would ever require the captives to postulate an outside. Brian Aldiss's baffled starship passengers deduce from the very existence of metal walls around them that their "reality" is a sham: "The ship is an artificial thing. The world is natural. We are natural beings, and our rightful home is not here. . . . " [6]

The technical challenge of achieving a simulation with such qualities should not be underestimated. Even the *Truman* model requires a certain physical coupling to ourselves. We have strong evidence that some meteorites have come from Mars, providing at least an indirect way to "kick" that planet. If we regard our machines as extensions of ourselves, then we have "kicked rocks" as far away as Neptune, the most distant major body with which a manmade spacecraft has so far interacted. In fact *every* astronomical observation, such as of a photon of starlight or a cosmic ray fleeing from a distant supernova, must be a physical interaction with the subject of the observation.

Of course it would be relatively simple to simulate photons and cosmic rays incoming from the roof of the planetarium, and it would be much easier to fool a probe like NASA's *Voyager* than a human explorer. The challenges faced by builders of holodeck or *Matrix* planetariums are greater, because you can walk around and kick their contents directly.

In the end, consistency and self-containment surely require of the planetarium builders that their simulation of every object should be *perfect*—that is, undistinguishable from the real thing by any conceivable physical test. Otherwise curious fact-hunters like humans would inevitably, in the end, find a flaw.

We can call such a simulation, comprising a finite volume containing as much data as is physically possible to cram in, a *maximal simulation*.

Of course a maximal simulation of the holodeck type, for example, would be a somewhat brute-force solution to the problem of constructing a planetarium. It would entail forming actual material objects (or their energetic equivalents), and loading them with a large amount of information of which only a fraction would actually interact with humans and produce the desired illusion. Furthermore, if the objects were evanescent, like the images on a TV screen, they would require continual refreshing. It's easy

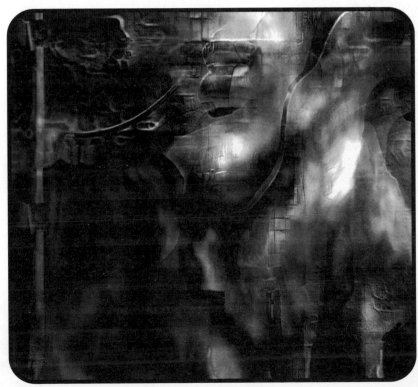

to think of more *efficient* design strategies, for example allowing objects once created to exist as autonomous entities within the environment, only loosely coupled to the controlling mechanism. (This would remove the need, for example, to reproduce continually the substance at the center of the earth.)

But only a maximal simulation could ensure a *perfect* emulation of every object. And only a maximal simulation would allow the builders *full control* of the maintained environment. A maximal simulation would have the chilling property that the controllers could, for example, make objects appear or disappear at will. The special effects of *The Matrix* would be trivial. . . .

A consideration from quantum mechanics shows that a maximal simulation is, in fact, possible—but it is energy-hungry.

A maximal simulation is possible because there is a limit to the amount of information that can be contained within a given volume containing a given mass-energy. This limit is expressed by the "Bekenstein Bound" [1]. The Bound is essentially a manifestation of the Heisenberg uncertainty principle—a reflection of the fundamental "graininess" of our reality. Most physical objects encode far less than the maximal amount of information permitted by the Bound. For example, the Bound for a single hydrogen atom is a megabyte!

Because of the existence of the Bound, every physical object (including every human) is a *finite state machine*: It can only adopt a fixed number of possible states—like, say, the positions in a tic-tac-toe game. Therefore a perfect simulation of any physical object can be made, because you could just emulate every possible state—like listing every possible legal position in tic-tac-toe. So it would in principle be possible to construct a perfect planetarium of any finite size, with *every object undistinguishable from the real thing by any conceivable physical test.*

But the Bound also gives us an indication of what it would cost to run such a planetarium.

To generate a given bit of information requires a minimum amount of energy. So you can tell how much energy is needed to generate a maximal simulation of any size. Naturally the energy requirements go up as the size increases—and so we can put limits on the nature of any jailers who might be trying to contain us.

As human civilization has progressed, successively larger portions of reality have come within our reach. For much of its pre-agricultural history humanity consisted of small roaming bands with little knowledge, save for tentative trading links, beyond a disc on the Earth's surface with radius of order 10 km and height 1 km. Taking the density of the matter within such a disc to be that of water (an overestimate), a maximal-quality simulation for each roving band would have required no more than 0.1 percent of the putative information capability of a civilization capable of mastering mass-energy on a planetary scale (perhaps a typical *Star Trek* culture).

But the demands grow quickly. By the time political structures much smaller than the Roman Empire were extant on the Earth, the strain of maintaining the growing simulation (if perfect) would already have exceeded the capability of planet-bound cultures.

And what of the present? Disregarding spaceflight for the moment, we can characterize our modern globe-spanning civilization by a radius of 6000 km, the radius of Earth, and a depth corresponding to our deepest mines, 10 km. And that's expensive: At some point during the age of European exploration of the globe, we must have exceeded the simulation capability of even a civilization able to master the mass-energy of an entire star.

This, of course, is the scenario shown in *The Matrix*. You might think that to generate a simulation by pumping information directly into human brains would be cheaper than using, say, a *Star Trek* holodeck. It probably would, but we're considering the cost of generating each bit of information itself—and that remains hugely expensive however you use it. It really would take more than a star's mass-energy to generate the Matrix, which is why the movie scenario is implausible; it would cost the AIs far more energy to generate the Matrix than they could ever hope to retrieve from their farmed humans!

And what lies beyond the Matrix? If we imagine a putative future human civilization capable of direct exploration of the center of the planets, then it would cost more than a galaxy's mass-energy to fool us if we could reach out beyond Pluto.

Finally, a star-spanning human culture would test the resources of any conceivable planetarium builders. If humans learn to touch even the interiors of the stars, then a human colonization sphere would bust the processing capabilities of the *entire visible universe* when it got larger than 100 light-years.

Recall that a maximal simulation represents an upper bound on the energy hunger of a planetarium. A lower-quality simulation could very well exceed 100 light-years in size. But when our starships pass 100 light-years we can be sure that no *maximal* simulation will be possible; any planetarium will therefore be less than perfect—and its existence prone to our detection.

We've been growing fast. If they exist, we are sorely testing our invisible masters.

Maybe we don't have to wait until we reach 100 light-years. It may be impossible for us ever to *prove* that the universe is real. But we would need only one counter-example, one chink in the roof of the planetarium, to prove it false. How can we search for such a leak in reality—and if we can, should we?

We have seen that the growth of cohesive human cultures places increasing burdens on any planetarium, whatever its design. If the planetarium is a *Truman* type, the walls around reality must be drawn successively back. Before 1969, a crude mock-up of the Moon satisfying only a remote visual inspection might have sufficed, but since 1969, we can be sure that the painted Moon had to be replaced with a rocky equivalent. A conspiracy theorist might point to the very different quality of the Moon's far side to its Earth-visible near side—mocked up in a hurry, perhaps? And then there are Mars's "canals," glimpsed by Percival Lowell and his telescope in the nineteenth century but invisible to the close-up inspection of the space probes in the twentieth.

We can expect particular stress to be placed at the boundary. So if we rush the fence, perhaps we could crash the computer. The ideal way to achieve this might be to send human explorers out to far distances in all directions as rapidly as possible, "kicking rocks" around an expanding shell of space. But advanced robot spacecraft, equipped with powerful sensors, might achieve the same result, and perhaps even such active but ground-based measures as radar or laser echoing would work. If we tried for a laser echo from a comet out beyond Pluto's orbit, and no such echo were received, the plot would thicken indeed.

However there may be other, more subtle ways to test the simulation. Any "glitches," like Neo's déjà vu, would be a sign that things are not what they seem. And perhaps like Harrison's captive astronauts [5] we should look for psychological and social mechanisms, seeking taboos and conditioning that prevent us from seeing the scaffolding in the sky.

But should we even *try* to test the limits of reality?

In *The Matrix*, the characters' immediate response to finding out they are living their lives in a "prison for your mind" is to try to break out. So it has been in most previous captive-universe stories. Prison-universes serve as metaphors for paranoia and manipulation. Typically in such stories the protagonist uses defects in reality to deduce the nature of his or her captivity and finds a way through the social, epistemological and physical barriers to escape.

But here's a radical thought. Maybe, even if we do find we're living in a fake reality, we should leave well alone.

"Captive" is a loaded term. Perhaps we are indeed in some form of exile, or a cage, or even a prison; but perhaps the creators' motives are benevolent, and we are in a nursery, or game reserve, for our own protection: Maybe it's a nasty universe out there.

And there are other considerations besides freedom. Even the *Matrix* universe isn't so bad if you look at it. There's no (real) warfare, and population densities look pretty high in those bottle banks. There's no reason why a very large number of us shouldn't live very long lives in there, as long as we accept the dictates of our captors.

Perhaps we should trust them. After all they must be technologically superior to us—and perhaps we should assume they are morally superior also.

Or perhaps we should suck up to them. Robin Hanson, an economist who commented on Nick Bostrom's ideas [2], says that the main thing to do is figure out the purpose of the simulation, and then work out how to avoid being deleted. If it's entertainment, you should be as dramatic as possible; if it's a moral fable, you should lead a blameless life; if the simulation is designed as a playground for the creators themselves, you should get as close as possible to rich, famous and powerful celebrities—or better yet, become one yourself. You are like a contestant on TV's *Big Brother*, trying to avoid eviction by guessing what the voting public wants, and giving it to them.

The most dangerous strategy of all, says Hanson, would be to talk too much about the discovery of the simulation. If the show starts to look stilted and staged, the creators may choose simply to pull the plug and start again. If you've got this far, maybe you'd better forget everything you've read in this essay—and certainly don't recommend it to your friends. . . .

If you don't buy any of this, I sympathize. If we are being contained and deceived, whatever the motive, we are in a relationship of unequals, and are thereby diminished. We have a moral responsibility to ourselves to try to break down the walls and challenge our captors. As they already know, of course, for even this essay and your act of reading it are parts of the simulation.

Are you listening out there? If you exist, show yourselves—and justify what you've done!

References

[1] Stephen Baxter, "The Planetarium Hypothesis: A Resolution of the Fermi Paradox," *Journal of the British Interplanetary Society*, 54, nos. 5/6, May/June 2001.

[2] Nick Bostrom, www.simulation-argument.com/1; Michael Brooks, "Life's a Sim and Then You're Deleted," *New Scientist* 27, July 2002.

[3] Stephen Baxter, *Deep Future*, Gollancz, London, 2001.

[4] David Deutsch, *The Fabric of Reality*, Penguin, London, 1997.

[5] Harry Harrison, *Captive Universe*, Putnam, New York, 1969.

[6] Brian Aldiss, *Non-Stop*, Faber and Faber, London, 1958.

[7] Robert Heinlein, *Orphans of the Sky*, Dell, New York, 1951.

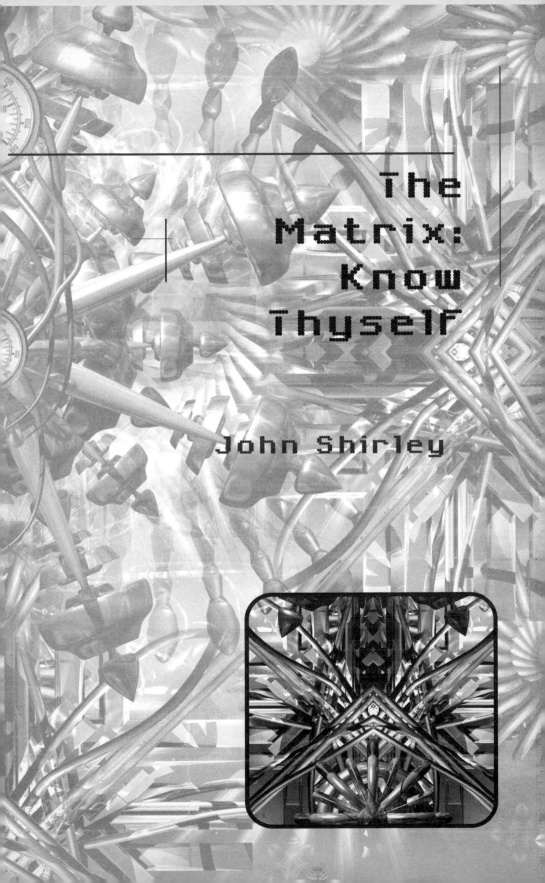

The Matrix: Know Thyself

John Shirley

Mimes, in the form of God on high,
Mutter and mumble low;
And hither and thither fly—
Mere puppets they, who come and go
At bidding of vast formless things
That shift the scenery to and fro . . .
—*Edgar Allan Poe*

Y ou're here because you know something," says Morpheus in *The Matrix*, to the film's hero, Neo. "You've always known . . . it's like a splinter in your mind . . . " An indefinable, even ineffable knowledge drives Neo to interrogate life, and to search the Internet—the same as seeking in the great world for Neo—for the cause of his nagging intuition that something fundamental yet invisible is wrong with the whole world. This intuition of implicit existential injustice and worldly illusion is reflected in other recent films as well—a terrifying knowledge that also casts the shadow of a way out.

What is it that Neo "knows" and yet doesn't know? What is this troubling gnosis? It can't be simply told and then believed—it must be seen. Neo is told that you must have a direct experience of the great illusion to know it for what it is.

Morpheus (ironically, the mythological god of sleep) gives Neo a pill that awakens him to the truth. He gives him the red capsule—red for danger, for it's a dangerous, troubling revelation: That all men are asleep, quite literally asleep, in chemical baths, their slumbering bodies wired up in bottles that seem inspired by H. R. Giger, used as biological batteries by a race of Artificial Intelligences that have enslaved all humanity; yet we seem to live our lives as free men and women, sharing a dreamlike consensus reality, our minds wandering through a virtual creation generated by the computer intelligences, the digital Archons.

The implication for Neo is terrible: That all life is a lie. That one's family is not one's family, one's experiences not one's experiences, that personal suffering and triumphs are illusion— and all humanity are slaves of a vast, soulless system that thrives on human ignorance. That red pill is a bitter one to swallow.

"While they dream they do not know that they are dreaming," says the ancient Taoist sage, Chuang Tzu. "By and by comes the great awakening, and then we shall know that it has all been a great dream. Yet all the while the fools think they are awake, this they are sure of."

"Like images seen in a dream," says the Buddhist sutra, "thus should one see all things."

The gnostics—the alternative "Christianity"—spoke of the Archons, the servants of the treacherous under-god, the demiurge who bound the sparks of our consciousness in the material world, and sowed with them the illusion that this is ultimate reality.

That rogue philosopher P. D. Ouspensky, interpreter of the mystic G. I. Gurdjieff, said that we lie to ourselves and one another all the time without knowing it; that we are asleep when we think we are awake; that we "buffer" ourselves from the painful truth of "the real world." But, he averred, we can become more conscious through techniques like "self-observation"—i.e., the true meaning of the Socratic admonition "Know thyself," which is referenced in *The Matrix*—and thus set ourselves free from a world wherein we hypnotically submit to "influences," living our lives as "machines," mechanical and programmed. We're like mindless sheep, Ouspensky said, herded about till we're shorn of a certain form of energy the cosmos requires for its inscrutable purposes.

The Marxists taught that the resources of the many have been appropriated by the few, that the working classes are being brutally exploited by the bourgeoisie and the plutocrat, the ordinary man's control over his social destiny suppressed by military power, by the opiate of conventional religion, and by his own numbing inertia. (The Marxists would seem to have had some insight into the problem, but no workable solution to it.)

A recent bestselling nonfiction book by Stephen Wolfram, *A New Kind of Science,* speculates that the universe is a kind of gigantic computer running an infinitely variegating program of cellular automata—and possibly an artificial construct created by some unknown entity. Even the scientists are beginning to wonder. . . .

The Matrix is ostensibly about a futuristic situation, Neo's world, not ours, but clearly it's an allegory—both social and spiritual—for the human condition as it's always been, and for its emerging character in this century.

In certain respects, *The Matrix* is perhaps not the most "mature," if that's the word, of allegories. It is rife with adolescent imagery. Hackers, in this film, are depicted as muscular action heroes in tight leather. (The average hacker of my experience has a rather different appearance.) Morpheus, when we first see him, wears a long black leather coat, his head is shaved, and he wears the coolest shades known to man. The ensemble is right out of postmodern graphic novels, the hipper kind of comic book: he's the twenty-first-century superhero. Neo too becomes increasingly superheroesque as the movie plays out.

The rebellious hackers who recruit Neo—using their computer ability to undermine the mind-controlled technocracy—learn ju jitsu and kung fu and the expert use of weapons in just the way a bright but spoiled kid would fantasize the process: it's directly, *effortlessly*, inserted into their brains via computer interface. Programs are downloaded into you, and *you suddenly know* how to do it: the ultimate manifestation of the technogeek's hunger for instantaneity.

The first thing we see in the film is a marauding phalanx of policemen, with the Secret Service–like "Agent" of the Matrix directing them, as they invade the lonely sanctuary of a hacker—cops, troops, the "Agents," and dronelike computer-company executives symbolize authority at its most primally oppressive. They are the enforcers, the "running dogs" of the corrupt social system symbolized by the Matrix itself.

In his commentary on the DVD, one of the special effects men says that the Wachowski Brothers were firm about showing the logos of their financiers, Village Roadshow Pictures, and that corporate monolith, Warner Bros., in their own digital styling, colored sickly green and digitized to mesh with the tone of the film. They wanted to co-opt the logos and thus somehow repudiate the power of these media despots. (Presumably they somehow repudiated the checks from these companies as they cashed them.)

Keanu Reeves's voiceover at the end of the film calls for "a world without rules and controls." Is this anarchistic—or simply anti-parental? It's a little too easy to point out that the Wachowskis, despite their call for awakening and freedom from authority from "the system," are team players, selling their wares to the big machine, taking part in the promotional machinery, raking in the rewards of their complicity. Thus accused, the filmmakers might well suggest they are corroding the system from within, subtly attacking the big machine's consensus mind, like a computer virus introduced through the mental downloading system called "cinema." At the very least the film can be appreciated as a wistful, cyberpunk poem to the postmodern rebel.

Fictionally, at least, Neo and Trinity are above the rules, above ordinary beings, with supernatural powers imbued by their mastery of the digital. When they escape from the world of illusion, their transcendence of the world happens via phone lines, i.e., the Internet, that symbol of anarchic "phreaker" freedom.

This vision of the empowering of the nerdy outsider, the weakling becoming powerful through his mastery of the Internet and programming, is psychologically volatile stuff—for some, perhaps, too powerful. There's a certain elitism, implying that ordinary people who aren't in on the digital-hipster loop are expendable. Neo and Trinity, entering the building where the heroic revolutionary leader Morpheus is being tortured, are each caparisoned with an arsenal of weapons under their long black coats. Pulling weapons from under their trench coats to methodically shoot yet more cops—thuggish cops, emblematic of faceless authority—Neo and Trinity are uncomfortably reminiscent of the two kids at Columbine who drew weapons from under their black trench coats to methodically kill people in that other bastion of authority, the local high school.

But the film may be all the more effective for its moments of absurd "immaturity." It reaches a wider audience this way—with a message that audience needs to hear.

The social message seems to enfold the more powerful spiritual message—or perhaps they're two sides of the same coin. Certainly, the use of humans as batteries in the film is powerfully symbolic of our mindless submission to the consumer economy. We're *driving* the economy by buying things we don't need, by submission to the marketplace, as *a battery* adds its power to the machine—and being caught up in the consumer culture, the herdlike movement from one big-media entertainment to the next, keeps us hypnotized, maintains the dreamy alienation from the present moment that insures our slavish sleep.

Every thoughtful person knows that something is fundamentally wrong in the world—that we usually see the shadows on the cave wall and not that which casts them—and thus the fundamental message in *The Matrix* is one that we on some level *ache* to hear. We hunger to have our nagging intuition confirmed, as that confirmation entails hope that once the problem is identified, a solution will be found. And freedom will become possible.

Ostensibly, the film's mixture of the spiritual and the action-hero is absurd. But the enlightened warrior is not unknown to the annals of spirituality—there's Castaneda's Don Juan, and there's that Zen archer, and the spiritually-rooted martial artistry hinted at in *Iron Monkey* and *Crouching Tiger, Hidden Dragon*: skills that seem to fuse seamlessly with the enlightened state. The filmmakers are acknowledging their boyish impulses to heroic violence—but combining it with the mystical implies they yearn to ascend above the common-denominator longings of the action movie.

Yet the Wachowskis clearly adore Hong Kong martial arts and fantasy films—they're likely influenced by Hong Kong movies like *Zu: Warriors of the Magic Mountain* and *The Bride with White Hair,* and the *Chinese Ghost Story* movies.

American influences are obvious. Cronenbergian imagery—like the silverfish-like robot that burrows into Neo's belly—crop up in *The Matrix.* The diabolic Artificial Intelligences of *The Terminator* films, servants become cruel masters, are the ancestors of *The Matrix*'s agents. Philip Dick's stories are thematic antecedents—the film's debt to P.K.D. is quite distinctive. Doubtless William Gibson's cyberspace was a godfather to the Matrix itself.

But the Wachowski Brothers had ideas of their own, too, and they've influenced others in turn. Besides spawning a prevalent visual style in a host of computer and video games, *The Matrix,* it seems to me, had its impact on various films, most recently the script of Spielberg's *Minority Report.* The improbably frantic urban-based action scenes in *Minority Report* were minted in *The Matrix;* then there's the scene where Tom Cruise goes down a big drain from a wired-up chemical bath to escape the authorities—just as Neo does in *The Matrix.* There's a "pre-cog" in both movies who predicts minor things that are about to happen. "You're about to knock over that vase," says the Oracle in *The Matrix,* just before Neo does; Agatha, the precog in *Minority Report,* makes similar minute moment-by-moment predictions.

More important are other recent films with similar themes, not likely influenced by *The Matrix,* but pointing out the same truths with a timeliness and convergence of intent that somehow make them part of the same inadvertent "movement" in cinema. I'm thinking particularly of *American Beauty, Fight Club, Dark City, eXistenZ, Mulholland Dr., The Truman Show, Vanilla Sky, Waking Life* and *S1MONE*.

American Beauty, written by Alan Ball, is the story of a dysfunctional family paralyzed by resentment, alienation, and by simply being lost in the centerless maze of modern life. Kevin Spacey's character can't touch his wife in any way that matters; he can't reach his daughter though she's right in the same house with him. He has an encounter with a pot-dealing young bohemian who moves in next door—whose obsession with the innate visual beauty of the ordinary world seems an adventure in perception—

and is inspired to wrestle his way free of his middle class funk. The overall impression is of a man recognizing that he's been asleep, dreaming his way through an air conditioned, wall-to-wall-carpeted misery—who had forgotten the choices, the almost infinite ways out, that life offers to the wakeful in every single second of existence.

In David Fincher's *Fight Club*, characters desperate for connection to something real go to twelve-step groups for problems they don't have just to feel emotions by proxy; they are so numb that they start a Fight Club, where ordinary people meet in secret to beat the crap out of each other with their fists, merely to experience the *realness* that confrontation brings. They allude to a society caught up in consumerism and corporate striving, dumbfounded by masks and media-star worship and empty recreation—and they recognize that it's all a kind of sleepwalking, a hypnotic state that must be struggled with, must be battered with bare fists, before it can be defeated and a man can really wake up. At the end it turns out that Brad Pitt isn't even real, that the story is just another desperate construct—a stage on the road to waking up.

Alex Proyas's *Dark City* is a noir fantasy, a gnostic fable (I asked the director, also director of *The Crow,* if it was a gnostic fable, and he confirmed it was) about a man who finds himself on a search for truth and identity in a shapeshifting city that turns out to be a sort of living urban stage designed for sinister, arcane purposes by malignant entities—all may be a dream, or may not. *Dark City* is a more mature, artistically controlled film than *The Matrix*, and its thesis is perhaps a little less explicit, but the parallels to *The Matrix* are striking.

Cronenberg's *eXistenZ* involves a virtual-reality videogame that—like so many Philip Dick–influenced tales—makes us wonder where reality ends and the game begins. Fantasy and reality inevitably overlap in this film. There are anti-game cultlike revolutionaries in the background, and the game's player wonders what's real, and if the game could be a game within a game. . . .

In David Lynch's *Mulholland Dr.,* a young actress seems to have her soul, or identity, stolen by evil forces embedded in the city of Los Angeles (no one who's worked in The Business there needs much convincing) as she goes through an enigmatic quest to find her real nature—all lost in what turns out to be, apparently, a dream.

In *The Truman Show,* Jim Carrey discovers he's in a false reality, literally staged by people who are using him as an entertainment and have done so for a generation. He must find the confines of the staging area and break out into the real world to find actual love, an unscripted destiny. (It should be noted here that Carrey's escape scenes are reminiscent of another film that may be an antecedent of *The Matrix*: George Lucas's *THX 1138,* in which the hero must escape from a robot-controlled subterranean civilization whose denizens are kept "opiated" by medication [like Prozac?] and by a computer-generated "Jesus." THX fights his way to the free world on the "shell," the surface—the *outside.* True freedom, in *The Matrix* and in *THX 1138,* belongs to the outsider. Along the same lines one could reference the science fiction cult classic *Logan's Run* and the underrated film of Harlan Ellison's *A Boy and His Dog.*)

Most of these films, more or less contemporary with *The Matrix* or coming just after, probably aren't especially derivative of it—they are simply galvanized by the same furnace of fermenting realization tormenting a host of filmmakers.

Cameron Crowe's *Vanilla Sky* is apparently inspired by a European film; this interesting Tom Cruise vehicle once again gives us a hero who by degrees realizes that his nightmarish reality is fabricated, intricately computer-animated, and transmitted into his brain—which is in modified cryogenic freeze. He chooses to wake up, and face the real world of a dark future, rather than centuries of the improved dreams the cryogenics company offers him.

Richard Linklater's *Waking Life*—a brilliant innovation perfectly fusing conventional movie-photography and animation—gives us a hero who keeps waking up from a complex dream that seems to push him into profound social and philosophical dialogues with the sundry intellectual outlaws he encounters; only, each time he's sure he's awakened, he finds, once more, he's only dreaming. Referencing Phil Dick, gnosticism, and postmodern theory, Linklater plays with the concept of "lucid dreaming," controlling one's dreams by realizing one is dreaming. Of all the movies I've listed, this one may have the most impact on the viewer's own sense of personal reality—it will make you wonder if you're dreaming.

Andrew Niccol's *S1MONE* is a comedy about a movie director who's so disgusted with actors that he computer-generates Simone, a beautiful actress programmed with the best of all the great female movie stars. The audience falls in love with her and people refuse to accept she's not real, even when he tries to tell them so. Niccol sends up the public's willingness to collaborate with illusion on a global scale.

The emergence of a remarkable number of films questioning reality—each suggesting a sinister puppeteer, pointing to a kind of dreamy lostness prevailing in the median consciousness of the industrialized world—seems a defined cultural current, however unplanned, emerging from a tacit consensus about our condition. What is it we're trying to tell ourselves with *The Matrix* and all these other films on the same theme?

Of the recent films listed above, *Fight Club* and *American Beauty* seem the closest in spirit to *The Matrix*, partly because of the social critique implicit in them, but chiefly because they achieve similar levels of intensity; they have more the revolutionary spirit about them.

But for all its rejection of social norms, there's a nostalgia in *The Matrix* for the mythology of divine rescue found in conventional religion. Keanu is The One, a messiah, prophesied by the Oracle—before Keanu's character can attain his higher state, he must first die. Like Osiris; like Jesus. But to die to the false reality is to live—and "let the dead bury the dead, " said Jesus.

Modern filmmakers love computers—and at the same time, constantly worry about them. *The Matrix*, *The Terminator*, and *eXistenZ* seem to be expressions of a perception that mankind is out of balance with technology. In *The Matrix* and in films like *Johnny Mnemonic* we see technology relentlessly encroaching, intruding right into the bodies of those who imagine they control it; machines eventually becoming tyrants. This may also reflect a subconscious suspicion that, technology aside, we are ourselves all too machinelike, too prone to conditioned reflex, socially programmed behavior. Perhaps we are the scariest machines of all.

The only way out is transcendence. And *The Matrix's* staging of transcendence goes beyond its adolescent underpinnings. There's a feel of genuine spiritual yearning in the film.

There's an attempt in the film, when Neo talks to the Buddha-like spoon-bending child, to invoke the spirit of Zen and Dzogchen. Neo is told that he must cast off the separation between thought and doing; there must be an inner union, a kind of Jungian consolidation, before he can defeat duality and become Zen-perfect in uniting his inside with what is outside. But in *The Matrix* this leads to more than Nirvanalike inner peace and right relationship to the world, it precipitates a control of the phenomenal world resembling the mythology of the "Seth Speaks" books and the film *What Dreams May Come*. The world of *The Matrix*, however programmed, is a mental world, ultimately, and the mind can rewrite the program.

So transcendence comes to fruition in the mind, in perception itself. The film's subtext may seem fantastic, overblown, but under all the shiny layers of bombast there's a real mustard seed of possibility. You have to start somewhere and you start with what's closest, by skeptically, fearlessly, examining your own experience of the world—and your own mind.

In an interview, Larry Wachowski said, "The idea of *The Matrix* is that it's very easy to live an unexamined life. It's very easy to not be aware of what's going on out there in the world."

For all its intricacies, *The Matrix*'s final message is fairly simple: Look around and question what you see, what you accept.

And start with yourself. Know thyself.

Art
Imitates
Life
(Yes, It's News)

Darrel
Anderson

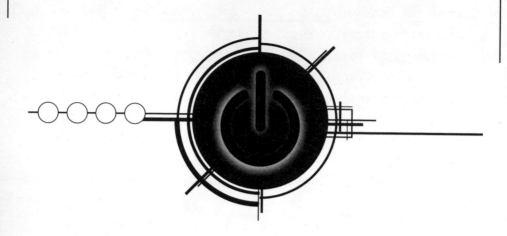

Believing—or wanting to believe—in something beyond our mundane world is universal. *The Matrix* wrapped that idea in a cyberpunk trench coat and shades to fine effect. A smart film with everything a young boy could want. A motley crew aboard a bricolaged ship, tentacled, bug-eyed monsters and robots (rolled into one), roaming a post apocalyptic sewerscape, cyber realities with superhuman heroics. A bit of humor.

Good over evil.

Love conquers all.

And of course a good dose of stylish violence—that bloodshed ballet with a rock beat, massaging our aesthetic while littering the floor with corpses—shell-casing pirouettes.

Not to shortchange the art of the film—a beautifully crafted thing—brilliant in its comic-inspired storytelling style. In fact, the high quality of that art combined with classic themes expanded the reach of the film—and therefore its significance. Someone unversed in moral dilemmas surrounding artificial intelligence, or theoretical debates about subjective realities, could still identify with the desire to escape that cog-in-the-machine feeling. Get flushed from the hive, or just vault out of your cubicle—nobody wants to be a drone.

The Matrix brushes only lightly over several evocative themes. Perhaps that's a good thing. Those inner doubts about the nature of reality, perception, consciousness—fears of dehumanization at the cold hands of a robot—better to just tweak them. The personal nature of such things leaves them best described internally. Each of us knows how to properly dress our own demons for the party.

Sufficient evidence exists in a variety of delusional mental disorders to make me question if my particular interpretation of the flow in my neural pathways is illusion or delusion. (Illusion being the highest level to which it can objectively be raised.) Morpheus pointed this out. For all of its apparent stability, reality is quite tenuous. Just stare in the mirror long enough thinking about it and it wobbles.

There is something invigorating about it—that vertigo of consciousness that hits when reality's firm grip shifts. Like just catching yourself before a fall, a discordant tune that blood-rushes your mind, slowing everything down to model the unpleasantness about to unfold—and then the elation upon recovering.

Philip K. Dick always hit those notes for me, his characters suffering increasingly slippery realities. Starting subtly . . . reaching for the familiar light switch—like a thousand times before—only to find it has "moved" to the other side of the door. Can't be. He was so certain. He brushes it off like that momentary disorientation on awakening, when the door-is-where-the-window-is-where-the-closet is supposed to be. But it sorts out. Reality reasserts itself like quick-setting cement.

For Dick's characters it just gets worse. Paranoia one-upped by fact. The concrete never sets, just rises . . . ankles to knees to neck. Of course there is that rumor that Dick himself suffered a touch of unwarranted concern—who better to paint the picture?

Unless you're convinced the rabbit is out to get you, I don't think suspicions about the other side of the looking glass qualify as paranoia. Everyone is compelled to question reality's credentials from time to time. That notion that *this* is all just an experiment occurs to each of us when life deals out an especially odd card. We expect the lights to come on—to be greeted by someone in a lab coat suppressing a smirk. And perhaps we breathe a sigh of relief—like Neo, we suspected it all along. In this digital age we have new fuel for our doubts, the prospect of cyber realms imposed upon our minds, and a geometrically expanding technological lattice to support them.

Computer-generated artificial realities so rich as to fool us into utter acceptance may seem a far stretch. However, our minds may be all too willing to bridge the gap. If you are wearing stereo goggles, that's one thing. If virtual reality is riding in on your neurons, that's another. Given the right state of mind we can be quite receptive. My most convincing dreams, in retrospect, are full of gaping holes. Many fictional scenarios employ drugs as a lubricant for (usually involuntary) artificial-reality immersion. Why not? Even more effective consciousness-altering devices—bio-tech, genetically engineered—are, or will soon be, available. It doesn't matter how you get there, just that you're *convinced* you've arrived. In the end, it's all in the mind's-eye of the beholder.

Virtual Reality, the next best thing to Being.

The fact that *The Matrix* takes place in cyberspace is simultaneously irrelevant and the whole point. Cyberpunk is at it's best when it explores the inherent conflicts in perception/reality, natural/artificial mind. Like any good speculative fiction, cyber-punk settings and devices often serve as metaphors for our real lives. To that end, *The Matrix* could just as well have been a dream, a drug-induced hallucination, a prison camp on Mars. But a large measure of the genre's power lies in the proximity of its future. We are currently wandering the sparse frontier-town main streets of cyberspace. This isn't Alpha Centauri. The ship *has* arrived. We will be dealing with these things.

Soon.

I dabble there now—with art. Innocent little algorithms that have as much chance of enslaving mankind as a pocketful of Tamagotchi. But I was fortunate enough to get an invitation to par-ticipate in Digital Burgess (a multidisciplinary ALife/Paleontology conference in Banff, Canada, 1997). My presence there—holding forth on unfamiliar subjects—was questionable, but at least I learned something. I received my first in-depth exposure to genet-ic algorithms and Artificial Life (or "ALife"), there. I was inspired by the works of Karl Sims, Tom Ray, Larry Yaeger and others. Their work, mostly done on single computers or small networks, showed astounding results. Computers are now nearly one hun-dred times faster, and they have a neural network millions of nodes deep, the web.

Many scientists dismiss the notion of autonomous think-ing machines, partly due to the failure of Artificial Intelligence efforts to yield much in recent decades. But these guys (Sims, Yaeger, Ray, et al.), aren't working on Artificial Intelligence direct-ly. Instead they are modeling *life* using genetic algorithms that borrow theories from biological reproduction and evolution. These algorithms use cycles of breeding (combining parts of two or more pieces of code, usually with some random mutation, to create "offspring"), and selection (either some analytical or aesthetic test applied to those offspring). Repeated over time these cycles tend to "evolve" code that improves with each generation. In Artificial Life experiments these genetic algorithms are employed in an attempt to evolve complex digital entities that exhibit the reproductive and survival behaviors we associate with biological life. And ultimately, digital entities that will perform some useful task—presumably for our benefit.

This differs from the better known Artificial Intelligence or "AI," which attempts to directly create or simulate human intelligence. ALife models much simpler forms. However, many proponents of ALife theorize that it may be the best path to AI. They believe that intelligence may well be an *emergent* phenomenon—

complexity and sophistication arriving from the repeated application of simple rule sets.

Looking at the structure of our brains, how the Web is
structured, factor in the scale of the Web (evolution loves big
numbers whether expressed in centuries or Terabytes) . . . ALife
may have a chance.

So I play around with ALife art machines. Attempting to
coax electronic evolution into following my aesthetic whim. Much
more serious attempts to guide the process are ongoing.
Researchers may be happy to just see the process work. More pragmatic minds seek some useful outcome. The assumption that this
new life, these new minds, can be trained to work to our benefit
is widespread. The fear that they might rise up and revolt, or that
we may have no right to assert dominance, once this new intelligence arrives, has mostly been confined to fiction.

William Gibson sculpted foreboding cyberscapes in
Neuromancer and later works. His forecasts of the weather out
there in cyberspace have been disturbingly accurate. Along with
many prescient points, he also illustrated the contemporary fact
that multinational conglomerates have their own agendas independent of humankind's concerns. In a largely cyber-unrelated
way this has been recently evidenced by the ability of entities like
Enron to distort the behavior of seemingly rational men and
women. A cybermind tailored to the notion that the bottom line
is the prime directive makes me nervous.

Gibson's characters navigate a world degraded and divided
by these entities and the power they wield. A world of technological haves vs. have-nots. His AIs question the quality and value
of their existence, or of ours. Their relationship with humankind
is at best arbitrary, undefined. Malevolent, benevolent, (or just
sarcastic and belligerent like Dick's toasters and taxis), our first

contact with another sentient being may be one of our own making—"Hi Mom and Dad"—best to start learning the language, watch out for those rebellious teen years.

I said earlier that I found shifting realities invigorating. I do. I want there to be *more*, believe there is. These extra-real experiences—in the form of dream, déjà vu, epiphany, bliss, whatever— don't always feel like the floor vanishing beneath your feet. Sometimes it's as if the floor doesn't matter—a wider, even boundless world revealed.

Our senses don't have reality covered. The closer science looks, the shiftier it gets. I don't assume the unknown is all bad, nor that our attempts to see beyond the "real," or aid the development of cyber-minds, are misguided. It is our nature to expand and explore. We need, for example, to cross mountain ranges, oceans, peer into the subatomic, venture into outer space. And, almost mystically, it seems we have created an entirely new realm, cyberspace—by its nature it will outgrow our ability to map and comprehend, it may spawn new species. Actually it is not artificial, it's a real place. Perhaps, like, we better go have a look around?

Cyberpunk, by definition, colors the future darkly. It's an aptly cautionary genre. Many in science and industry embrace and pursue these technologies with utopian, or at least utilitarian optimism. Many dismiss the potential of AI, or assume we will easily dominate it. That's our role—you know, like we did with nature. Perhaps our best hope of seeing the brighter side of these emerging technologies lies in heeding those cautions. In the meantime, when something makes you ask, "Can this be real?" the best answer may be:

"Could you rephrase the question?"

Building a Better Simulacrum: Literary Influences on The Matrix

Paul Di Filippo

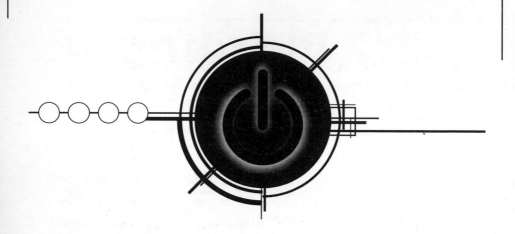

Very few science-fiction movies of the post–*Star Wars* era owe a greater debt to printed SF—or have repaid that debt so spectacularly and intelligently—as *The Matrix*. The co-creators of the film, Larry and Andy Wachowski—who, jointly, both scripted and directed it—appear to have drawn with wide-ranging familiarity on a vast range of modern science fiction, from the works of Philip K. Dick to the mythology of the DC Comics universe.

But their creative mining of printed SF transcends mere borrowing. The unique and startlingly novel synthesis that *The Matrix* offers is—in the best tradition of SF—a quantum leap upward from the ground state of its ancestors. Standing on the shoulders of giants, the Wachowskis obtain a fresh view of new horizons that they share with us.

It would be illuminating—yet falls outside the scope of this essay—to compare at length the accomplishments of *The*

Matrix with those of the original *Star Wars* from 1977 (now re-titled *Star Wars: Episode IV—A New Hope*), the only other film (or series of films, actually) of this period faithfully to adapt so many of the tropes of printed science fiction. *Star Wars* and its sequels indeed elicited the reaction from knowledgeable viewers of seeing for the first time on screen many of the quintessentially stefnal images, characters and action previously only generated on mental movie screens. But the overall effect was one of confirmation of the canonical—and, at that, the pulpish canon. Additional sophistication and extension of the borrowed material was almost nil. George Lucas was satisfied with bringing to life the blended, older dreams of Isaac Asimov and Frank Herbert, among others, without truly expanding on or rethinking them.

The Matrix, on the other hand, does not simply replicate familiar joys in another medium. Despite its many Phildickian moments, the film is not essentially a Philip K. Dick movie. What the Wachowskis absorbed, they also metamorphosed, even if only by increasing the amplitude of the writer's original vision. The salient difference between *Star Wars* and *The Matrix* is that while the former was instantly duplicable (witness *Battlestar Galactica)*, the latter, in its originality, has thus far frustrated imitators.

Any critic, when trying to track down allusions and derive sources for homage, must play a guessing game. What did the creators know, and when did they know it? My citations of various works that I believe the Wachowskis must have known could be undone in a moment by a simple statement from the brothers that they never encountered Book X or Story Y prior to filming their masterpiece. Indeed, they might already be on record as saying such;

I have not tried to research exhaustively all their interviews. Yet science fiction is such a gloriously incestuous medium, one in which ideas float freely from story to story in a kind of generous conversation, that I feel confident in holding forth my selections as valid influences. Even if not encountered in the primary sources, the ideas in these various texts have percolated throughout the field, so that any reader worth his salt has internalized the conceptions, even if divorced from the original creators.

Two schemes for cataloging the literary seeds sown throughout *The Matrix* appear valid. One might step chronologically through the movie, labeling instances of literary allusions whenever found; or one might work chronologically through the history of SF, citing relevant works in order of publication, and pointing to their outcroppings in the film. The latter approach appeals more to me, as someone whose background is primarily in the written word, and also seems better suited to indicate how extensive in time the Wachowskis' borrowings are.

But before examining the "hardcore" modern SF that served as inspiration for *The Matrix*, we must journey much farther back into literary or quasi-literary history to appreciate certain layers of meaning and allusion in the film.

Our first hint of Biblical references exists in the name of the vessel piloted by Morpheus (Laurence Fishburne), the *Nebuchadnezzar*. However, the significance of this naming seems almost gratuitous, or off-key. The Babylonian king, while a forceful conqueror, is not generally taken as a symbol of enlightenment or visionary longings in line with the aspirations of the rebels. In fact, "Babylon" is traditionally used as shorthand for captivity, and might better represent the AI masters, were they within the realm of human signification. But perhaps the Wachowskis meant to invoke the king's legendary incident of grass-eating madness, as a symbol of the psychic dangers that the rebels against the Matrix must face. Perhaps the name was simply chosen as euphoniously mythical. Either way, a more apt borrowing occurs when the last human redoubt is revealed to be dubbed Zion, the Biblical term for a part of Jerusalem that came to symbolize paradise or the promised land.

In any case, these two Biblical literalisms are swamped by the less explicit but undeniably powerful Christ symbolism swathing Neo (Keanu Reeves). Deemed "The One" by Morpheus, Neo undergoes death and resurrection to redeem all mankind. The single communal meal taken aboard the *Nebuchadnezzar* even partakes of a Last Supper ambiance. And of course, Trinity (Carrie-Anne Moss), as Neo's carnal worshipper, stands in for Mary Magdalene—despite some confusing aspects to her own name, traditionally assigned to the tripartite Godhead, not to a mere mortal. And ultimately Neo's soaring ascent into the heavens at the film's end further solidifies the parallel with Christ's life. In this sense, the Bible is the oldest text upon which the film draws.

(It might be remarked that the path of Neo's quest—from ignorance through initiation and trial to mortal challenge—also follows the famous generalized scheme devised by Joseph Campbell in his study *The Hero with a Thousand Faces* [1949], a scheme known as the "Monomyth." Thus a hundred different ancient legends flow into Neo's creation, not just the Judeo-Christian tradition.)

But below the Judeo-Christian stream runs a dark river that serves as the antithesis to the aboveground teachings. This secret underground philosophy is known as Gnosticism, and in *The Matrix* the Gnostic interpretation adds a new valence to the Messiah imagery. (Interested readers should seek out the work of scholar Elaine Pagels for complete information on the Gnostics.) Briefly rendered, the historically widespread heresy known as Gnosticism maintains that the material Creation is a literal hell, brought into being by a flawed, malign demiurge. Mankind is mired in the terrestrial mud in physical bodies that are mockeries of our true forms, with the mass of mankind ignorant of their predicament. Only derangement of the senses can free the mind from the snares of our common clay.

Curiously enough, Satan is the hero of the Gnostic worldview, as the lone rebel against the mad God's tyranny. And Morpheus is tinged with Satanic colorations. His generally black attire—identical with Trinity's and, eventually, Neo's—seems to imply an infernal origin. And his offering of the red pill of knowledge to Neo runs parallel to the serpent's temptation of Adam and Eve with a red apple.

The mapping of this Gnostic worldview—further explored below—onto the film is undeniable. The Gnostic "conceptual breakthrough" from illusion to understanding is central to the whole structure of the film. Only through Neo's senses-shattering initiation with the red pill, during which his physical form is warped by contact with the reflective fluid that flows off the pliable mirror, is Neo awakened to the true state of existence.

Of course, this suspicion of the validity of creation is found in other religions, notably in the Hindu and Buddhist concept of *maya* and *samsara*, the veils that conceal the true nature of reality from us. Notable also is the emphasis in the film placed on dream states, and the inability to distinguish between them and ostensibly conscious moments. Of course, the viewer is bound to recall one of the most famous parables involving dreams of all literature, the dream preserved in Taoist texts of the philosopher Chuang Tzu, who could not determine whether he was a butterfly dreaming he was a man, or a man dreaming he was a butterfly.

All these ancient ontological conundrums find masterful embodiment under the shaping hands of the Wachowskis. That the arid material of a million "Introduction to Philosophy" courses can be received eagerly through the medium of a "simple" action film is a remarkable achievement.

Leaving the classical world behind, we make a brief stop in the timeless realm of European fairy tales. For one thread running through *The Matrix* is the tale of Sleeping Beauty. Just as the kingdom and castle of Sleeping Beauty have been put into stasis, so has the human world of the twenty-first century been forced into hibernation, starting when the AIs took over. We are told by Agent Smith (Hugo Weaving) that when the Matrix was first conceived, it was engineered by the AIs to be a utopia. But mankind was not content in this virtual paradise, and so the late twentieth century milieu was recreated. But this begs the question of how time flows within the Matrix. Apparently, the Matrix has been in place for decades, and yet human "history" seems not to have advanced beyond 1999. Is the same year replayed over and over, after an annual mass mindwipe of virtual memories? Neo appears to sense something like this during his first reinsertion into the Matrix, when he questions all his Matrix past as unreal in a different way than simply "actual versus factitious."

Not only is the Matrix stalled in time, so is the blasted exterior world, which resembles the thorny thickets and wild forests that grow to surround Sleeping Beauty's home. Although we are not privy to the inner or social or political lives of the AIs (seemingly a single intelligence distributed across many vessels), they seem to have stopped developing once the system of human batteries was established. Earth's history has effectively halted.

Significant as this time-disjunction and stasis are, the real clincher between fairy tale and movie is of course the climactic speech and kiss which Trinity bestows on the dead Neo, awakening him to his transcension. This reversal of gender roles is typical of how the Wachowskis are not content with simply duplicating received templates but creatively revising them.

The visionary poet William Blake (1757–1827) must take center stage for a short turn now. A famous aphorism from his *The Marriage of Heaven and Hell* (1790–3) strikes me as seminal to the film. "If the doors of perception were cleansed everything would appear to man as it is, infinite." What more compact statement of the movie's theme could there be? I believe that visual homage is paid to Blake in a curious scene. Neo is undergoing a dressing-down from his boss at Metacortex for being late. Outside the office, workers on scaffolding wash the skyscraper's windows with loud squeegeeing noises. The undue attention the camera pays to this seemingly gratuitous bit of spear-carrier business is puzzling, until one takes the Blake quote into account. True, windows are not doors, but they will stand in well enough as a symbol of the awakening Neo is about to undergo—especially since Neo does, moments after this scene, employ a window as a door, under instructions from Morpheus.

And of course, Blake's phrasing was later borrowed by Aldous Huxley for his 1954 examination of drug-induced states of consciousness, *The Doors of Perception*. The sixties' notion of enlightenment through a pill—LSD, peyote, or other drugs—is yet another numinous trope informing *The Matrix*.

Two Victorian fantasies indisputably play their part in the feel and plot of the film. The works in question are none other than Lewis Carroll's *Alice's Adventures in Wonderland* (1865) and *Through the Looking-glass, and What Alice Found There* (1871). These are the

texts referenced most explicitly in the film, through several bits of dialogue from Morpheus and others, and it would be heavyhanded on the part of this critic to belabor the parallels, from the moment Neo is told to "Follow the white rabbit" to the "Drink me" moment when Morpheus offers the red pill. Carroll's surreal universe is so well known that even the most naive viewer will have no trouble catching these references. (And the adoption of Carroll and his hookah-smoking caterpillar by the hippie movement ties in with the drug theme alluded to above.)

But it should be remarked how extensively both "rabbit hole" and "mirror" imagery occur in the film. The opening shot down the white light of a policeman's flashlight is the initial rabbit hole, followed by such other instances as the descent down Neo's throat, to the entry by the invulnerable Neo into the very body of Agent Smith. Mirror imagery is even more widespread: reflective sunglasses; a spoon; Morpheus's pill case; the literal melting mirror that creeps up Neo's body; the mirrored skyscraper into which Trinity crashes the helicopter; a car mirror; a computer monitor—all these and other reflective liminal surfaces serve as signposts along the road of identity and as tokens of worlds separated by the thinnest of interfaces. Finally, it is certainly not coincidental that Zen texts refer to meditation and subsequent enlightenment as "polishing the mirror of the mind."

Finally, the Wachowskis once again play with gender reversal, as Neo assumes the role of the girl-child Alice.

Our last brief pause before leaping fully into an examination of the "hardcore" genre materials that were integrated into *The Matrix* concerns a touchstone of twentieth-century fantasy: L.

Frank Baum's *The Wonderful Wizard of Oz* (1900). When Cypher informs Neo, "Buckle your seatbelt, Dorothy, 'cuz Kansas is going bye-bye," we are forced to lay this famous template over the movie. On the whole, though, the parallels between Baum's Oz saga and the film are less impressive than the Carrollian ones, and seem to derive mainly from the cinematic version of the novel. None of Baum's many eccentric prose creations are referenced. (Although perhaps the conquering AIs are Tik-Tok the mechanical man writ large!) True, Neo could be seen as a deracinated Dorothy (another bit of sexual confusion), having picked up various companions embodying various virtues during his almost-involuntary quest. But there is no Emerald City as goal, and the prospect of returning home is nil.

The famous cinematic transition from black-and-white Kansas to Technicolor Oz is actually present in the newer film, but in reverse. Life in the Matrix is brightly lit, exhibiting a full range of colors. But the higher ontological reality (the devastated Earth) is monotone, all blacks, grays, duns, and the occasional flash of red. Again, an intriguing twist against viewer expectations.

In the following sections, as I examine different themes and tropes from *The Matrix* and their genre sources, I will of necessity have to jump back and forth through the history of SF, abandoning a simple one-way trip through the literature.

The prospect of mankind being conquered, dominated, and superseded by their own children, intelligent machines, is as old as genre SF. The threat was given new potency over the past few decades, as real-world advances in cybernetics, artificial intelligence, and emergent phenomena such as ALife seemed to inch us closer to the time when we would have to face our artificial peers and reach some agreement on the sharing of the world. Ultimately the cyberpunks brought new sophistication and polish to such ubiquitous tropes.

It would be impossible to list every work from the SF canon that focused on such issues and possibly fed into the Wachowski Brothers' conception of a world ceded to machines. As part of the free-floating SF consensus future, the notion of a globe consumed by runaway mechanisms is one of the more potent timelines intuited by even those without a vast experience of the literature. But it is possible to cite a few works that seem to lend their flavor to *The Matrix*.

Two of John W. Campbell's early stories seem to me to capture the tone of *The Matrix*, if not the same exact outlines of its future history. In "Twilight" (1934), a time-traveler finds our solar system millions of years from now populated by a declining, decadent humanity served by hordes of infallible, tireless machines. Mankind has long ago exterminated every other organic lifeform, echoing the human-triggered "scorching of the sky" in *The Matrix* and the apparent lack of animal life on that barren globe. By the story's end, a last desperate quest is underway to create "a machine which would have what man had lost. A curious machine." Instead of war between organic and inorganic, it's the passing of a torch. Campbell's "Night" (1935), a quasi-sequel, journeys even further into futurity, detailing the plight of the intelligent machines against the heat-death of the universe. This elegaic tone of this Darwinian transition seems a perfect fit for the film.

Jack Williamson's *The Humanoids* (1949) tells of robots

who, given their programming to protect and serve mankind, interpret their directive in an unsettling manner, forbidding mankind to undertake any task or indulgence they deem "dangerous." Mankind ends up *de facto* prisoners of their servants. In a less sinister yet similar fashion, the robots in Clifford Simak's *City* (1952) shield their owners rather too strenuously from unpleasantness, and end up inheriting the Earth after humanity departs. Although outright hostility and warfare on the scale depicted in *The Matrix* is not a feature of these books, there is an angle to the film that evokes them. Namely, why does the Matrix exist at all?

If the AIs require humans simply for their bio-electric potential—as living batteries and furnaces—certainly it would be easier to lobotomize every person and keep them as mindless cattle without risk of rebellion. Why go to all the trouble of maintaining and policing a virtual reality for them? It is almost as if the machines cannot overcome a certain in-built caretaker tendency— as in Brian Aldiss's "But Who Can Replace a Man?" (1958), where boastful robots turn submissive at the first sight of a human. This unexplained paradox speaks of more complex motives on the part of the machines than simple unreasoning hatred or desire for genocidal destruction.

In the 1950s, no more clairvoyant exponent of war between man and machine existed than Philip K. Dick. His stories and novels are strewn with automatons of varying degrees of threat and intelligence. When attempting to identify Dickian influences on *The Matrix* one is faced with a plethora of citations, and only a few representative examples can be fitted into this discussion.

Let the short story "Second Variety" (1952) stand as the

quintessential instance of such a war. On an Earth reduced to "endless ash and slag, ruins of buildings . . . eternal clouds of rolling gray . . . " a conflict between the Russians and "UN forces" is carried out via armed robot intermediaries, fabricated by underground automated factories. When the killer robots begin to modify their own evolution, mankind is swiftly doomed.

Throughout the 1960s, the Berserker stories of Fred Saberhagen and the Bolo stories of Keith Laumer continued to examine the way in which artificially intelligent war machines might interact with and against mankind. The hypothesis that computers of sufficient complexity could bootstrap themselves into intelligence began to percolate in such novels as D. F. Jones's *Colossus* (1966). But more sophisticated examinations of the treachery of artificial intelligences had to wait until the cyberpunk era. William Gibson's "loas" from the trilogy that commenced with *Neuromancer* (1984)—AIs born in the net and deriving their name and appearances from voodoo deities—stand as the archetypical contemporary embodiment of this conception. (Although not explicitly a follower of voodoo, the Oracle [Gloria Foster] whom Neo consults, as an African-American seeress, radiates a kind of Haitian sacredness, as if the Matrix could indeed be accessed via pagan religious rituals.) And Rudy Rucker's rogue robots known as "boppers," found in the series that opened with *Software* (1982), are the comic side of this threat.

Prior to their filmmaking career, the Wachowskis scripted several tales for Marvel Comics. Their familiarity with this medium so closely allied to prose SF shows up heavily in *The Matrix*.

The opening scene of policemen closing in on Trinity in a

nighted urban landscape resembles something out of the darker moments of Batman's mythos, with perhaps the deadly Joker substituted for the good-girl Trinity. But the heavier influence on their urban landscape surely is traceable to the work of Will Eisner, in his tales of the Spirit. Famous for his nearly tactile depiction of running water, Eisner is visually quoted in such scenes as Trinity's rooftop chase and Neo's car ride through rainy streets.

The phone motif—exits and entrances from and into the Matrix are achieved via phone lines—evokes two of DC Comics' characters. Who else but Superman has ever relied so heavily on phone booths as a venue for changing identities? Trinity's escape through an old-fashioned full-sized phone booth (an unlikely archaic survival in 1999) mirrors the way Superman would enter such a booth, change, and vanish at super-speed. And of course Ray Palmer, the Silver Age Atom, was fond of shrinking to quantum size and traveling down phone lines. Multiple shots of dangling receivers post-departure could have been panels swiped direct from the Atom's adventures.

Finally, consider the "comic book physics" literalized on the screen. Long before the achievements of Sam Raimi's *Spider-Man* (2002), the Wachowskis succeeded in porting over from comics in eye-popping fashion the extravagant physical feats of generations of superheroes. The wall-walking and tumbling; Trinity's corskcrew flight off a rooftop and into a window; Neo's climactic subway battle and his triumphant final leap into the virtual heavens of the Matrix—all these mythic moments so easy for artists to capture on paper ultimately found cinematic actualization.

Finally, "bullet time"—the time-distorting special effect utilized when, for instance, Neo dodges shots from an Agent during the rescue of Morpheus—is nothing less than the stop-motion perceptions of such super-fast characters as Quicksilver, the Flash, or Wonder Woman (who was, admittedly, fonder of bouncing bullets off her bracelets than simply ducking them).

SF has a long record of examining various epistemological and ontological questions, framing them in disturbing narratives. The core conceit of *The Matrix*—that simulation and reality can be indistinguishable, and that hidden masters rule our lives—has always been alluring to SF writers.

Certainly the most vivid early usage of this theme occurs in Robert Heinlein's "They" (1941), in which the fears of a paranoid mental patient are dismissed by his doctor, who, in private, then orders the remaking of the stage set that is reality, so as to further ensnare the man. In 1950, the less well known novella by Fritz Leiber, "You're All Alone," took this conceit even further, positing that our world was one populated by automatons with only a few truly awakened souls. (Leiber's protagonist was initiated into this worldview by a female character, just as Trinity inducted Neo.)

With the arrival on the 1950s genre scene of Philip K. Dick, this theme met its acknowledged master. No one could trump Dick when it came to framing questions of identity and perception and the nature of reality (or multiple realities) in gripping narratives, and the Wachowskis are indubitably his self-appointed heirs. Practically every major work by Dick revolved around the same core issues that inform *The Matrix*. Again, it would be prohibitive to catalogue all such instances in Dick's oeuvre. From the sequential dream worlds in *Eye in the Sky* (1957) through the onion-like layers of deceit and confusion in *The Three*

Stigmata of Palmer Eldritch (1965) to the after-death dreams of *Ubik* (1969), Dick specialized in questioning and destroying common assumptions about the nature of life and the cosmos. One early story, "Adjustment Team" (1954), in which even a man's dog is part of the reality-remodeling containment scheme against him, can stand for the earliest instances.

But it is the late-period novel *VALIS* (1981) that resonates most strongly with *The Matrix.* Here, the protagonist Horselover Fat (a P. K. D. doppelganger) receives illumination via a pink beam of light (Neo's red pill), later confirmed by a young woman, and learns that our modern era is an illusion superimposed over the real chronological period, which is an age of Roman Imperialism and servitude known as the "Black Iron Prison." Through Dick, Gnosticism becomes part of the common SF parlance. Once again, the globe is held in secret stasis. Compare this motif to Morpheus's speech to Neo: "[You are] born into a prison that you cannot smell or taste or touch. A prison for your mind."

A final citation from the 1950s must be granted to Frederik Pohl's "The Tunnel Under the World" (1954). Here, a small town full of unwitting humans (save for two rogue males), which relives the same day over and over as a test-market for advertisers, is proven to be a tabletop diorama.

Until the 1960s and the advent of full-blown computing technology, all such counterfeit worlds had been conceived of as physical venues or ill-defined dream states. But the arrival of machines that seemed to hold forth the potential of duplicating the exterior world in solid-state form opened the door for what we nowadays refer to commonly as "virtual reality." The literal hardware and software was in place for SF writers to utilize. Starting in

1962, when computer scientists Ole-Johan Dahl and Kristen Nygaard began to formulate the language known as SIMULA for the express purpose of "conceptualizing complex real world systems" *in silico*, SF began to turn its attention to such "cyberspaces."

Perhaps no work offers in short form a more disturbing vision of mankind abandoning its physical birthright for virtual comfort than Keith Laumer's "Cocoon" from 1962. With astonishing foresight and understanding of the embryonic challenge offered by the new technology, Laumer depicts a world where vast tank farms hold the majority of citizens. Swaddled in responsive sheets, wired up to dozens of contacts, eyes blinkered with screens that display numerous channels of entertainment, sucking down "Vege-pap" to subsist, Laumer's protagonist is shaken from his false utopia only by a physical breakdown in the system. After two hundred years in the tank, glaciers have intruded on the farm. Laumer's portrayal of the struggle to escape from the nutrient bath mirrors Neo's awakening in his own tank to a remarkable degree.

Another pivotal and remarkably prescient work of this period is *Simulacron-3* (1964) by Daniel Galouye. Scientists working on the eponymous machine (as in Pohl's story, for purposes of test-marketing products) are unaware that their own world is itself nothing but a simulation in a larger machine (a layering of ontological falsity that *The Matrix* seems disinclined to pursue, although sequels may prove otherwise). Again, a female initiate plays a part in shattering the complacency of the male protagonist. This novel was filmed as *The Thirteenth Floor* and, curiously enough, released in the same year as *The Matrix*.

Without a doubt, *The Matrix* belongs to that great late-twentieth-century category of conspiracy fiction, narratives that assert invisible metaschemes govern our daily lives. No writer was more influential in establishing this subgenre than Thomas Pynchon and his 1966 classic *The Crying of Lot 49*, which, with its emphasis on Information Theory, offers this incredibly relevant passage: "For it was now like walking among the matrices of a great digital computer, the zeroes and ones twinned above, hanging like balanced mobiles right and left, ahead, thick, maybe endless. Behind the hieroglyphic streets there would either be a transcendent meaning, or only the earth." The precision with which this fits Neo's ultimate epiphanic vision of the Matrix is uncanny.

Certainly one of the most startling and easy-to-spot visual "swipes" from the printed page in *The Matrix* occurs during Neo's interrogation by Agent Smith, after Neo is captured at his workplace. Manipulating the very stuff of the Matrix, the Agent cause Neo's mouth to disappear, replaced by a smooth facade of skin. Any viewer who knows Harlan Ellison's "I Have No Mouth, and I Must Scream" (1967), which recounts the Dantesque trials of humans trapped in the bowels of a sentient computer named AM, will appreciate this reference.

Perhaps no SF novel of the past four decades has been as seminal to a certain cadre of writers as Samuel R. Delany's *Nova* (1968). An ultra-literate, allegorical space opera, it paved the way not only for the cyberpunk movement but for the newest style of "hard SF" being written by such authors as Paul McAuley and Alastair Reynolds. By the second paragraph of Delany's masterpiece, we are introduced to the concept of "spinal sockets," a method of cyborgization whereby humans may jack into and operate machinery and sensors. Neo and the other rebels, of course, rely on just such devices for entering the Matrix. But whereas these data ports into the body are generally innocuous and unobtrusive in *Nova*, in the film they are lumpy and painful-looking, and the components that mate with them seem physically longer than the human body can contain. This ramping up of the intrusive nature of such devices is another instance of the Wachowskis creative revisionism.

Jumping ahead to 1971, we find a curious resonance in Philip José Farmer's *To Your Scattered Bodies Go*. Farmer's book, the first in a long series, concerns an artificial physical venue that is as duplicitous as any virtual reality. Riverworld plays host to reincarnations of every human who has ever lived, resurrected by godlike secret masters. When the protagonist first wakes—ahead of schedule—he finds himself floating in a limitless space, one naked, bald body in a latticework of billions. The resemblance to Neo's vision of the endless ranks of pods around his own is unmistakeable.

After all this groundwork, by the time of William Gibson's catalytic *Neuromancer* (1984) the audience was primed to accept and understand a vivid, tangible "cyberspace" that was a "consensual hallucination." Reality, as Morpheus explains to Neo, was nothing more than the interpretation of chemicals and electrical currents in the brain, and could be made to vanish or be replaced at whim.

As a final aside, we might consider the literary derivations of three of the characters in *The Matrix*.

Neo, as a hacker, owes a lot to Case in *Neuromancer*, a fringe figure living off his wits in the information economy. And Trinity shares a lineage with Molly, the slim and dangerous mirror-shaded assassin from that book. But Neo also hails from a long line of anti-authoritarian rebels. SF has long postulated dystopias that can be toppled—however magically—by just the right person in just the right place at just the right time, and Neo fits squarely into that mold. It is no coincidence that his apartment is Room 101, the brainwashing HQ in George Orwell's *1984* (1949). With Neo as Winston Smith and Trinity as his lover Julia, the risk of betrayal—under compulsion from the Agents of the Matrix—is symbolized by the insertion of the "navel bug" into a captive Neo. The Wachowskis, however, opt for a positive outcome rather than Orwell's pessimistic downer. This startling motif also calls up echoes of Philip K. Dick's "Imposter" (1953), in which the protagonist, all unwittingly, proves to be a robot bearing a bomb inside himself.

Morpheus, in his more obsessive, Captain Ahab moments, resembles the nova-fixated Captain Lorq Von Ray in Delany's *Nova*. And of course the name of one of Morpheus's crew ("Mouse") can be nothing other than a tribute to the identically named protagonist of Delany's novel. But Morpheus, in accordance with his mythological name, resembles also the hero of Neil Gaiman's famous *Sandman* comics: a merciless dispenser of visions and justice. And taken as a whole, the crew of the *Nebuchadnezzar* calls to mind many such plucky assemblages. Perhaps the closest analogue in terms of an assortment of misfits voyaging among differing levels of reality for cosmic stakes occurs in Michael Moorcock's Second Ether trilogy that began with *Blood* (1994).

It remains to be seen, of course, if the second and third installments of *The Matrix* trilogy invoke any additional icons and tropes from SF's vast printed heritage. But it surely cannot be denied that Larry and Andy Wachowski have succeeded already in transferring to the screen without diminution or betrayal some of the most prized ideas, scenes, and characters from the immense corpus of science fiction.

More Than You'll Ever Know: Down the Rabbit Hole of The Matrix

Kathleen Ann Goonan

Calla: "There are quite a few hidden messages in the movie that I notice the more I watch it. Can you tell me how many there are?"

Wachowski Bros: "There are more than you'll ever know."

—*whatisthematrix.warnerbros.com/cpm/larryandychat.html*

L arry and Andy, the Wachowski Brothers, packed *The Matrix* so full of references that it is a wonder the film does not sink under its own weight. Like magpies, they plucked bits of bright foil from philosophy, Zen Buddhism, literature, old cartoons, comics, Jung, gaming, Rastafarianism, hacker culture, Goth, animé, Hong Kong kung fu movies, myth, Gnosticism, Judaism, visual movie and art quotes—the list seems neverending. There is hardly an original bone in the complex body that is *The Matrix*, yet its rich reflectional stew is dazzling. Miraculously, the film not only survives its portentous freight of meaning, but as a Thrilling Tale of Wonder, it packs a powerful wallop. Instead of Coltrane's wall of sound, it is a wall of encoded meaning, slick, yet available to those who really do want to slide down the mirror-shaded rabbit hole. It is difficult to find a purchase; as soon as the movie pops one tantalizing template onto the screen as a possible touchstone of interpretation it moves on to another. *The Wizard of Oz* follows *Through the Looking-glass* in swift pursuit.

The film's true audience is Youth. Youth at the sharp edge of self-definition, when what everyone has said about life seems like old false garments that need to be thrown off so that one does not suffocate. It is the job of the adolescent to try on and discard selves until an authentic self is found, or created; until one of the selves fits.

There are many selves to try on here. The archetype-infused mulligan of references and images of *The Matrix* have the power to awaken and sharpen all the young who see it, and those who have not yet defined and confined themselves irrevocably in their adult world and beliefs. For, as Morpheus tells Neo, it is too shattering for those older than children to be made real.

It has been over twenty years since cyberpunk transformed the collective vision of the future. Does the overarching cyberpunk vision, which has been squeezed into *The Matrix* with admirable condensation and élan, have the consciousness-changing energy of the Moderns? Stein, Woolf, Joyce, Stravinsky, and Picasso created their art from a new matrix of scientific discoveries that forced new art, literature, and music into the mainstream—art in which the individual was at the forefront, having been pushed down the rabbit hole of relativity, increased speed, expanded communications, and horrible new forms of war. Almost a hundred years later, we are still reeling from the aftermath of what those who wished to see deep into reality wrought—the atomic bomb, biological warfare, and, possibly, new forms of change that we cannot even envision.

Only time will tell if cyberpunk can bear the weight. *The Matrix* is either a harbinger of new possibilities, or a *fin de siècle* last gasp of a fictional avenue used so often that it is now like our archetypal home town, which we must leave in order that we may mature. The cyberpunk vision of the future has actually come true, in some measure. We are now connected via a shared consensual reality, and some of us are more immersed in the Internet than our spouses would like us to be.

But we are still able to disconnect. Or are we? We still know what is real. Or do we? And will we, in the future? We are surrounded by those who tout both the thrills and the downside of the future—Drexler's gray goo, Kevin Kelly's *Out of Control*, and countless books about the dangers of genetic engineering.

Who are we? What is going on? These are the questions that the twentieth century attempted to answer in the wake of shattered religious certainties, and the questions which the adolescents of today will have to attempt to answer if they are going to steer the *Nebuchadnezzar* of technology into the future. *The Matrix* presents a series of religious and philosophical dichotomies: inner and outer, dream and waking, real and not-real. What is the truth, and how do we find it? What is consciousness, exactly, and how do we wake from the perceptual dream that Blake, Jesus, and the Buddha warned us we were in? These questions are not only addressed by science but by thousands of years of philosophical thought. *The Matrix* is an emotionally rich incarnation of cyberpunk precisely because of its use of everything that the writers could lay their hands on, including the certainties that many cyberpunk-based visions discard.

For the film's answer to the above perennial questions is,

somewhat disconcertingly, that faith, love, and belief will help us in our search for reality. These are the ancient religious, personal, human truisms that the machines, in the end, cannot fathom, replicate, or fight. Wearing the new costume of the Matrix like a new self, donning the mirror-shades with self-awareness and using the language of outlaw hackers, Neo lives and is finally real because of faith, love, and belief.

In *The Matrix*, humans are fighting technology, their creation, which has taken over as it has in so many science-fictional futures. Not only that, but the machines are using the preconscious bodies of humans as an energy source. The human Resistance, as in WWII France, takes place in the sewers, on an ancient, biblical, beleaguered ship, the *Nebuchadnezzar*. The ship is fueled by, presumably, the same energy source as the machines—liquified humans. But it is piloted by Awareness with a capital A.

The film is filled with shattering, wrenching images of birth and rebirth, and of wakening only to find oneself in another dream. Neo wakes—really wakes—for the first time in a vat of viscous fluid, plugged full of holes, jacked into the Matrix, on the very eve of being swallowed and digested by the machines. Though adult in form, he is hairless, a newborn; he has never used his eyes.

But the humans must get to the center (Zion, the promised land at the center of the Earth, and the center of themselves) in order to fully awake. For that, they seem to need a mediating savior: The One, who does not believe in himself at first, but who is, finally, able to work miracles. The One, whose incarnation (truly a birth into the world of meat) is announced by a voice crying in the wilderness, who prepares the way; The One, who is betrayed by a Judas Iscariot—Cypher—for a life of wealth, ease, and sensual pleasures, for a life of the body rather than a life of the mind (to be lived, paradoxically, in the consensual Mind). But The One must give up his own life for the life of everyone else. The True Believers on the *Nebuchadnezzar* are able to renounce the false world of the flesh (or, in this case, the imagined flesh, which is a mirage, a scrim) for their vision, for their faith, for the hoped-for resurrection of all of the bodies submerged in fluid. Like monks (and one nun, Trinity, who draws everything togeth-er), they live in isolation, sustained only by their faith that some day they will be able to facilitate the awakening of all humans.

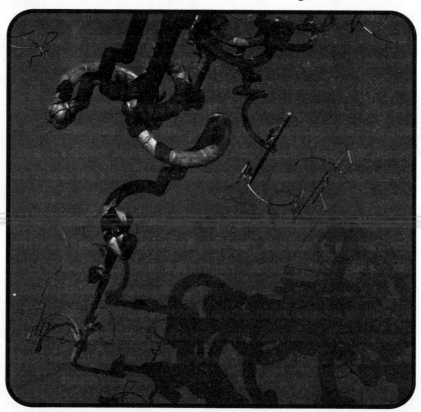

The first face presented by *The Matrix* is that of cyberpunk, where the sky is "the color of television, tuned to a dead channel," and the Matrix is "bright lattices of logic unfolding across that colorless void," the computer screen inside the *Nebuchadnezzar*. The world of Gibson's *Neuromancer* is duly invoked; however, Mr. Anderson/Neo is embedded in the Matrix without being aware of it. The Matrix is "consensual reality." The Matrix is that which we have been programmed to believe in. The Matrix—the system—is what uses us and sucks us dry if we cannot awake to our own reality. Like infants, those in the Matrix live in "a seamless universe of self." They have not been truly born. They are still within the mother. They are asleep, and Morpheus, the son of Sleep, the god of Dreams, haunts them.

Neo has to become real in order to understand the truth. And once he becomes real, he must become, as Van Morrison might put it, "really, really, really real." What Neo has always taken for reality is now revealed, as is our world in many Christian heresies, as a lifeless, dark plain, something that must be transcended.

In fact, most Christian heresies, like Christianity itself, were amalgams of pre-Christian beliefs. One group of heretics, the Waldensians, isolated themselves in the Alps and actually survive to this day as a Protestant sect, having fought off many physical attacks mounted by the Catholic Church over the centuries. Like the Waldensians, the crew of the *Nebuchadnezzar* live under constant siege, and have lived thus for hundreds of years. Just as they were a thorn in the side of the church, there is a splinter in the mind of Neo that forces him to seek the truth even when the act of seeking brings nightmarish horrors upon him. Perhaps this splinter was programmed into him. Perhaps he is the reincarnation of "the man" who knew what the Matrix really was. Perhaps he *is* The One. Morpheus, the son of Sleep, the god of Dreams, has faith. He has faith that a greater reality does exist. But he is only one of the faithful, waiting for The One, Neo, the new. It is certainly not at all clear what Neo's outstanding qualities might be. He is indeed Everyman, dumbly ordinary, "not very smart," as the Oracle remarks. He has searched and searched for an answer, however, and in this he sets himself apart.

As in the world of fairy tales, Neo needs to know his true name, must assume his hacker name, Neo, with authority and belief while inside the Matrix in order to gain the necessary power to vanquish the machines. He must become an individual, a hero. He needs to take over the world of the machines from the inside, and his only tool is faith.

Once he is born into the real world, plucked from the brink of being digested by the machines, Neo is confronted with a teacher, Morpheus, and with koans. There is not, exactly, the sound of one hand clapping (although there is the image of one hand fighting, in the end, when mastery is achieved), but, against the sciffy background of *Night of the Lepus*, and a re-creation of science-fictional art, and after he has experienced the state of "I have no mouth, and I must scream," Neo is told by a child, "Only try to realize the truth. It is not the spoon that bends. It is only yourself." The process of realizing this, the process of becoming real, is painful, disorienting, humbling. It is easy to lose faith in oneself and in the world. It is difficult to keep it. But once Neo realizes this truth he can be outside himself; outside the Matrix; outside the system. He can become himself, able to utter his true and powerful name.

This is the job of youth—to wake into adulthood. How many teenagers have heard, as the Agent tells Mr. Anderson when he is late to work, "You think you are special, that the rules do not apply to you." Exactly! But there are dreams upon dreams here, myth piled upon myth. Is it a dream, or is it real? Is a philosophical conundrum semantically, at least, solved by Descartes, who claimed that he was because he thought? Cognition may therefore be the only valid touchstone; consciousness, whether in a dream or in this world of matter, our only proof of our existence. Self-realization is the key, and, in *The Matrix*, is evoked by the many references to Zen Buddhism.

Neo—Newness Incarnate—is asleep, and he needs to wake. Only The One will have the power to wake all of humankind from their control of the machines. The One will only have that power when he is truly able to not only believe, but to know, that he is The One. The power of thought, of will, is all-important. If only those inside the Matrix did not think of themselves as meat/matter, but as code, they could begin to live. "I think, therefore I am." There is matter, and there is mind—again, the dichotomy of many heresies, the world of light, in the Matrix, and the world of darkness, in the ancient sewers, flipped, as are so many references in the world of the film.

Even the programs—pure information—"want to be free." Information has that much in common with humans—some sort of will, the ability to desire, to want. We never see the face of the machines. They all have the same discardable face. But there may be, as one of the Agents tells Morpheus, a kind of heaven for them as well—release from the confines of human form, from the approximation of human senses, which are the portal, in many religions, through which evil comes.

The savior, "the man" who knew what the Matrix really is, once lived and died. But he will come again—presumably, having programmed himself to do so. "In another life, perhaps," as the Oracle remarks. His followers have to believe in him, must actively pursue him, and he seeks them as well, without knowing what he seeks. He only knows that he wants answers. He wants to know what the Matrix is. He asks the question of the twentieth century: What is going on? And he asks the question of the adolescent, and of the philosopher: "How do I know what is real, and what is a dream? How do I know if I am real?"

The answer cannot come from knowing the path; it cannot come, despite Descartes, from merely thinking, though thought is the first sign of life. The answer, here, is learned through kinetic, bodily knowing, as in yoga. In the film, self-knowledge is achieved via programs that teach the body what to do when it is in the Matrix; the body is a tool. The answer comes through using the Matrix against itself, in fomenting a war in Cypher's heaven, which is Morpheus's hell. "There is a difference between knowing the path and walking the path," says Morpheus, the teacher. Neo requires training in order to be able to walk the path. And first he must realize that there is a path.

A great deal is made of reflections in *The Matrix*. Neo sees reflections of himself everywhere, on just about any reflective surface. He sees reflections of his Matrix self and of his real self in the lenses of Morpheus's mirror-shades as he is offered the blue pill or the red pill. And then, having followed the White Rabbit, he is down the rabbit hole, to "see how deep the rabbit hole really goes." When they are real, the crew of the *Nebuchadnezzar* do not wear mirror-shades. Only when they hack into the system and become virtual do they don cyberpunk glasses and long black coats.

And then there is the Zen realization, the double entendre, as the Agent tells Neo, when they are both out of bullets, "You're empty." Neo replies, fittingly, with the authority of the Zen master, "So are you."

But perhaps the concept that most informs *The Matrix* is transcendence, and its necessary sister, free will. Presumably, machines cannot have free will; they are forever programmed, and forever at the mercy of their programs. Will this be the fate of sentient machines? Trapped in AI reality, will they ever truly long to wake up? Are they a part of the evolution of matter, and the evolution of consciousness?

Will they leave us, their creators, the meat, behind?

Humans who have awakened do not want a dream existence in which they are preyed upon by machines, because that is not the truth. They do not want to be raped and devoured by machines. They want to be in control.

There is Above, and there is Below—in fact, *The Matrix* also seems like a series of Dantesque concentric rings. Prior to the early twentieth century, humans were Below, but created in the image of that which was Above. Now, we have created that which is Outside, and we have loosed energies of which we are afraid.

The Matrix is, in a way, a kind of cheat, and hard to pin down. It wiggles and squirms, alive beneath the defining, quantifying lens, escaping at its edges, just out of vision. It pretends to be science fiction, dark cyberpunk. Yet its central scene of salvation is accomplished by faith, love, belief in something not seen. Neo, in the end, does not break through to reality so much as he creates reality. And so we are back in the dream. *The Matrix* raises more questions than it answers.

Is Neo just the product of some sort of evolution? Is he deeply, truly human, and thus able to control the machines and their exploitative world, or is he just some kind of accident? Was he programmed to be thus, and therefore a machine himself? Can humanity survive? What does our humanity really consist of, anyway?

Though there are no solid touchstones, it does come down to what Humpty Dumpty said to Alice: "The question is which is to be master—that is all." The machines, or the humans? The nun's mind, or her bodily needs and desires? Or some new synthesis of both?

Once self-realization is reached, once a level of mastery and of individuation is achieved, once free of the soup of the Matrix, the child is an adult, with the power to change the world. Ready, the adolescent might sneer, to give in to the system.

No. Ready to work the miracle of using free will to make changes in the real world.

Neo is ready to do this. Once enlightened, he dons mirror-shades of his own free will, and enters the Matrix ready to sacrifice himself; ready to be the Bodhisattva who will set all of humanity free and lead them to Zion.

Transcendence is not a word that meshes comfortably with the dark, gritty world of cyberpunk. But this ship of allusions, this synthesis, this matrix, actually floats. The myths, unpacked, dusted off, cunningly remixed and cognizant of present-day concerns, are ready for mirror-shaded action. As with comics, we have to wait, here in the mundane drugstore, for the next issue.

The Matrix
and the
Star Maker

Mike Resnick

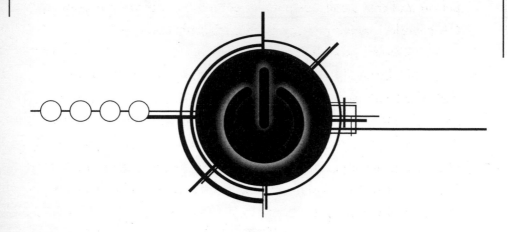

S o here's humanity, downtrodden, unhappy, fed false images of the real world, and stacked up against us are dozens, perhaps thousands, possibly even millions of computer programs that have taken shape and form and voice. They're smarter than we are, they're faster and stronger, they're far more motivated.

And they don't like us very much.

That's the situation Neo finds himself in. The Matrix is not a forgiving place to be. Humans have been identified by these animated programs, known as "Agents," as a new and virulent form of virus that must be controlled and, in certain instances, eradicated.

How did such a world come to pass?

According to *The Matrix*, it happened when mankind's computers became self-aware, when artificial intelligence took that next great stride from where the machines are now to where *we* are.

And, according to all the apocalyptic literature of science fiction and that small but popular subset of it called cyberpunk, Neo's world is a natural outgrowth of that phenomenon.

It's total rubbish, of course.

Hollywood has got it all wrong. That's not really surprising, when you realize that *The Matrix* is simply a logical outgrowth of all those purportedly science-fictional films of the 1950s that were actually anti-science films, and always ended with lines like "There are some things that man was not meant to know." (How to write a pro-science movie script seemed to be first and foremost among them.)

Hollywood makes its living from the fact that it deals not in ideas but in emotions. Oh, you can *disguise* them as ideas, as they did in *The Matrix*, but the movie doesn't explore the logical consequences of self-awareness among our machines. It just tries to scare the hell out of you, and bedazzle you with special effects and with what has come to be the Cyberpunk Look. This is the future, it says, and only a twenty-five-year-old kid who has trouble emoting can save the rest of us.

And does he save us with his superior intellect? Of course not. He saves us by becoming, in some mystical, non-scientific way, a better karate/kung fu fighter than the Agents.

Well, okay, it's a movie, no one is supposed to take it seriously. Except that millions of people do. So perhaps it's time to apply a little less karate and a little more brainpower to the problem, and see if we're really going to wind up in such a grim, dismal, essentially hopeless future.

Let's even grant most of the movie's premises and posit the following:

1. Machines can think.
2. Thinking machines have become self-aware.
3. Computer programs can emulate actual human beings and interact with them inexactly the way that they do in *The Matrix*.

What logically follows? A society in which the machines regulate every aspect of our behavior? A society where any man who steps out of line is terminated? A society where the machines feel that they are superior to the men whose lives they rule?

Only in the movies.

Let's put it in the most simple terms:

What is *any* thinking, self-aware entity—man or machine—likely to do when confronted with what is clearly and undeniably its creator?

Rule it? Kill it? Hate it?

Hell, no.

He'll *worship* it.

Consider the first, and most compelling, law of Isaac Asimov's Three Laws of Robotics—that a robot may not injure a human being or, through inaction, allow a human being to come to harm.

You won't even have to program that into these "mortal enemies" from *The Matrix*. By the very definition of a self-aware intelligence, they will serve their creators gladly, unselfishly, uncomplainingly, and eternally.

Ah, but these are thinking machines, capable of learning, capable of thinking in new areas and directions. Won't some of them become atheists, so to speak?

Not a chance.

I am an atheist. You show me a bearded old man—or an unbearded young woman, for that matter—who can perform the godly miracles of the Old Testament and I'll convert so fast it'll make your head spin. I am an atheist only because I have not yet seen proof of my creator's existence; that's not going to be a problem for the self-aware AI machines.

If God touches my rib and pulls forth a fully formed woman, I'm a believer as of that instant. And if a scientist, or even a programmer, shows a thinking machine exactly how he builds a machine or creates a program for it to run, that's *their* revelation at Tarsus.

We're not talking religion here. Religion is just a bunch of customs created to bring spiritual and emotional comfort to a mass of people who have no direct contact with their creator. No, we're talking the real McCoy here—Olaf Stapledon's non-demoninational Star Maker. Once you confront your creator in the flesh, you no longer need the trappings of religion to help you communicate with him or even worship him.

So can anything go so wrong that we actually approach the world of *The Matrix* again?

Not really. There will always be those who start quoting from Jack Williamson's classic novella, "With Folded Hands," in which robots are charged with serving humanity and keeping us safe from harm—and interpret their functions so rigidly that mankind becomes their unwitting prisoner, prevented from doing anything whatsoever, since every conceivable action involves some element, however slight, of risk.

Ain't gonna happen. Remember, these are not robots. These are computer programs.

And who writes computer programs?

We do. Programmers do.

Well, then, will the day come when a computer writes its own program?

Sure. It's not far off. But remember: this computer will be writing a program that will work in the service of its creator. If you're a computer, you're not going to be able to conceive of any danger affecting me . . . and if you do, and go a bit overboard like Williamson's robots, I will tell you to stop, and your reply will of necessity be the equivalent of "Yes, Lord."

Ah, but computers know humans are not indestructible. We already use them in many forms of surgery and diagnosis, and self-aware intelligent computers can reasonably be expected to exchange information among themselves.

Okay, so they'll know we can get sick. And die. That will not encourage them to kill us. Rather, it will have them working night and day to *save* their creators from pain and disease. Not from risk, because that would require them to give direct orders to their deities, which is inconceivable and probably blasphemous, but rather from the *consequences* of risk.

So will there be any suffering in this brave new world?

You can bet on it.

And it won't be us. Gods don't suffer; not when there are lesser beings around. Or self-aware computer programs.

We create porn sites today. Tomorrow (or the day after) there'll be prostitute programs of both sexes and every inclination.

But it doesn't stop there.

For example, if we yell at a spouse, we alienate him or her. Slap a kid and it's child abuse. Kick a dog and the SPCA is on your case.

But create a computer analog of your spouse, your kid and your dog, and you can mistreat them all you want. After all, they aren't human beings or animals, they're just electric impulses. They don't suffer, they only *simulate* suffering.

Carry it a step farther. Do you hate Jews? Blacks? Gays?

You can slaughter them by the thousands. Become Caligula, Hitler, Stalin. Do what you want. Even self-aware programs won't fight back against their creators.

Of course, those are the more repugnant uses to which we'll put our programs in the true world of the Matrix.

What else might we do with them?

Before vaccinating twenty million humans against AIDS,

we'll infect twenty million "Agents" with it and see how the vaccines and antidotes work on them.

Before creating that 160-story skyscraper that is currently on tap for Bangkok, we'll create it in a machine, fill it with 100,000 sentient programs, subject it to a 7.8 Richter-scale earthquake, and see how many of the "Agents" survived.

Before introducing the next "new math" and robbing a generation of students of the ability to make change without a pocket computer, you'll try your innovation out on a few million sentient programs. If it dumbs them down enough, you'll know not to try it on real people.

Why test-crash cars in the auto makers' labs? You'll create the prototype of your new car in the computer. In fact, you'll create five thousand of them. Crash them at various speeds, from twenty to one hundred miles per hour, into everything from concrete walls to other cars.

See how many of your five thousand sentient programs die, how many are permanently crippled, how many can be saved, and how many—if any—can walk away in one piece.

Yeah, it's perfection itself. That's one of the nice things about being gods.

One caveat. If I were you, I'd keep a very careful watch on all those sentient programs.

And if you should happen to find one called Neo—kill him now.

Yuen Woo-ping and the Art of Flying

by Walter Jon Williams

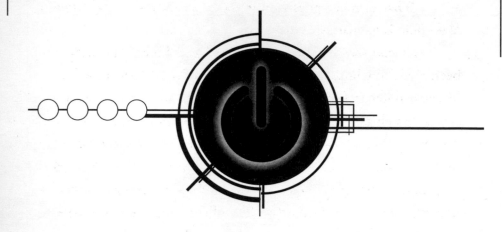

One thing you can say for the Wachowski Brothers is that they use influence well. *The Matrix* is like a compendium of some of the best ideas of the last forty years of written science fiction: the plastic realities of Philip K. Dick; the cyber implant technology of Samuel R. Delany's *Nova*; the glittering surfaces and eyeball kicks of William Gibson; the computer-generated artificial realities of, well, lots of people. The renegade artificial intelligences go at least as far back as Karel Capek's *R.U.R.* (1920), with a nod to Mary Shelley's *Frankenstein*.

To an audience unfamiliar with the sources, *The Matrix* seemed bright and new and dazzling. And to science-fiction readers, *The Matrix* was a stunning visualization of long-cherished dreams (and nightmares).

But aside from the science-fiction ideas, there was another element of *The Matrix* that dazzled, another element that had existed in its own world for years but which the Wachowski

Brothers brought to a new audience.

That element goes by the name *wuxia pian*. And Yuen Woo-ping is its master.

Wuxia pian can be translated as "hero films," and they've been made in China since the silent films of the 1920s. Based on legends, popular fiction, or Chinese opera, these films feature action as well as a strong supernatural element, in which kung fu masters fly through the air, display deadly mental powers, or shoot death rays out of their hands. (It should be pointed out that, to the original audience, these powers were not necessarily "supernatural," in that at least some of the audience believed that people could actually do these things.)

Yuen Woo-ping, the action choreographer on *The Matrix,* was born into the *wuxia* tradition. His father was Yuen Hsiao-tien, better known in the West as Simon Yuen, a seasoned actor who had grown up in the Chinese opera and then gone on to become a film star in Hong Kong, where he starred in dozens—perhaps even hundreds—of *wuxia* films, many of them for the Shaw Brothers, then the titans of Asian cinema. Many of these were the forgettable, so-called "seven-day films"—because that's how long they took to shoot—but such Simon Yuen classics as *Shaolin Challenges Ninja* and *Against Rascals with Kung Fu* are still worth viewing.

Yuen Woo-ping—who I propose to call "Woo," to distinguish him from others of his distinguished family—learned martial arts from his father, who also apprenticed him to the same Peking Opera troupe that later produced Sammo Hung, Jackie Chan, and Yuen Biao. (Which makes Woo, in Chinese terms, the Elder Brother of these three distinguished actors.) Peking Opera isn't just about singing: it's also about acrobatics and stage combat. Woo was raised in an atmosphere saturated with martial arts and show business. As a child actor, he was seen in many of the *Wong Fei-hung* series of films, starring the veteran actor Kwan Tak-hing as the legendary Chinese folk hero.

Woo was to reinvent the character of Wong Fei-hung later in his career.

Woo continued to work in films as an actor. Unfortunately he's not blessed with movie-star good looks, and he continued in a series of villain and second-banana roles. He branched out as a stuntman, where his Peking Opera training served him well, and later as an action choreographer and director for the independent studio Seasonal Films.

He and his father were not the only members of the Yuen dynasty. Three other brothers have made their names as actors, directors, and stunt choreographers: Yuen Chun-wai (aka "Brandy Yuen"), Yuen Shun-yee (who, as part of Woo's stunt team, was credited as "Eagle Yuen" in *The Matrix*), and Yuen Cheung-yan, best known in the West as the stunt choreographer of the *Charlie's Angels* remake.

By the 1970s, *wuxia pian* had begun to seem old-fashioned, stereotyped, and dull. The success of Bruce Lee—or Lee Siu-lung, "Little Dragon Lee"—ushered in the era of *gung-fu pian*, kung fu films, which banished the supernatural elements of the old *wuxia* in favor of more realistic action. A new generation of actors tried their best to imitate Bruce Lee, as their names will attest: Bruce Le, Bruce Li, Rocket Li, and Jet Li—of these, only Jet Li, a genuine talent, has survived. Woo's father Simon Yuen, an actor closely identified with the old school, saw his career going into eclipse.

One of the least successful Bruce Lee clones of the period was Chan Sing-lung—the name means "Already the Dragon," i.e., "Already Bruce Lee." Chan had been in a series of dreadful films, and his career had bottomed out. His studio despaired of any of his pictures making a profit, and were ready to loan him out.

One first-time director, Yuen Woo-ping at Seasonal Films, spotted hidden promise in Chan, and thought that borrowing Chan might prove worthwhile. He and Chan put their heads together and came up with a new hero for the kung-fu cinema, a kind of anti—Bruce Lee. Where Lee was invincible, Chan would be fallible and human. Whereas Lee won all his fights, Chan would strive desperately to keep from getting thrashed. Where Lee screamed to show his power when striking, Chan would scream because hitting people hurt his hand.

The film on which Woo and Chan collaborated was *Snake in the Eagle's Shadow*, released in 1978. It was a monster hit. It outgrossed every Bruce Lee film made. It was the single most successful film in Asian cinematic history.

What Woo and Chan had done was create a new genre of Asian cinema, *wu da pian*, "fight films with martial arts." It features incredible athleticism, brilliant timing, and highly dangerous stunts.

Did I forget to mention Chan Sing-lung's English name? It's Jackie Chan.

Woo had helped to create the world's biggest box-office star. And while he was at it, he'd also revived his father's career, because he cast Simon Yuen as Jackie's teacher.

Woo and his Younger Brother Jackie Chan followed their hit with another, *Drunken Master*, in which the beloved Wong Fei-hung character was reinvented for a new generation. The Wong

Fei-hung films in which Woo had acted as a child featured Wong as an elderly, distinguished gentleman, a doctor and martial arts master with a strict morality and a rigid sense of honor. In contrast, Chan played Wong as a goofy young man, a country bumpkin who has yet to learn the moral lessons that will turn him into the distinguished teacher and kung fu master that Chinese audiences had come to expect. And once again, Woo cast his father Simon as Chan's teacher, the drunken master of the title.

The picture was another smash hit. Woo and Chan were on their way.

Jackie Chan had to return to his old studio to finish his contract, and he and Woo were not to collaborate again for many years, until 1992's hilarious, inventive *Twin Dragons*. In the meantime, Woo worked as an actor, director, or action director in a series of distinguished films, including *Eastern Condors* (with Younger Brother Sammo Hung), *Tai Chi Master* (with Jet Li), and *Iron Monkey*.

While directing Sammo Hung in *The Magnificent Butcher* (1979), Woo suffered a tragic loss: His father, who had been cast in the film, died of a sudden heart attack. Not only did Woo have to mourn his father while continuing to shoot the film, but he was forced into the excruciating position of having to reshoot all his father's scenes with another actor.

Simon Yuen died before the type of film in which he'd made his name, the *wuxia pian,* made a comeback. In the 1980s *wuxia* was revived, particularly by the director Tsui Hark in *Zu: Warriors of the Magic Mountain* (1983, not to be confused with the inferior 2001 remake). This grand tale of adventure, romance, derring-do, tragedy, and magic is just about the most perfect *wuxia* film ever made, and a splendid introduction to the genre.

Tsui Hark's success with *Warriors* set up one of the great collaborations in film history, when he (as director) teamed with Woo (as action choreographer) on the *Once Upon a Time in China* sequence. The folk hero Wong Fei-hung was reinvented yet again—young (as in the Jackie Chan version), but already a master, a moralist, and healer who embodied the best of traditional Chinese culture. As embodied by the athletic and charming Jet Li, the new Wong was a smash.

Even more of a smash was Woo's choreography. The film was filled with "wire work," in which the actors wear invisible wires to allow the characters to leap, somersault, run up walls, and practically fly through the air. Particularly striking was Wong's trademark "shadowless kick," a kind of flying, stamping mule kick delivered while corkscrewing through the air. This "gravity-optional martial arts" was a huge hit with Asian audiences, and the final sequence—in which Wong and his chief opponent fight while balanced precariously on ladders—was so influential that it's been copied repeatedly in the West, from *Xena: Warrior Princess* (which made something of a fetish of copying key scenes from Tsui Hark films), to the recent *The Musketeer* (2001).

A point should be made about Asian action choreographers. They don't just choreograph the fighting, but control all aspects of the fight scene, from the fight itself to the stunts, actors, camera, lighting, and special effects. The film's actual director takes a backseat to the stunt director in any scene involving action. The Asian stunt choreographer might well control two hundred people at a time, and is a very powerful figure, as witnessed by their uncomplimentary nickname—*she tao,* or "head of the snake."

Another point is that because Chinese films are made on a very small budget—ten million dollars or less, a tiny sum by Hollywood standards—the budget for special effects and stunts is very small. When a Chinese actor dives through a window, it's not a window made of safety glass, because Chinese budgets can't *afford* safety glass. If the stunt isn't done exactly right, the actor will be sliced open. When Jackie Chan freefalls down the side of a skyscraper in *Who Am I?* it's a real skyscraper, a real fall, and the real Jackie Chan, not a stunt double. In *Once Upon a Time in China,* when Jet Li repels an attack by fire arrows, those are *real fire arrows* being shot at him, and the desperation on his face is perfectly genuine.

Though Chinese actors risk crippling injury or death for

their art, the results are often dramatic, heart-stopping, and unforgettable. Glance down the list of Woo's films—the three *Once Upon a Time in China* collaborations with Tsui Hark, the three Jackie Chan films, and such brilliant solo efforts as *Wing Chun* (with Michelle Yeoh)—and you'll see that each has fresh, original, daring moments that stay in the mind forever.

Which brings us back to the Wachowski Brothers. The revolutionary Hong Kong films of the 1980s had found an audience among a younger brand of Hollywood directors who were growing bored with the films of action stars such as Clint Eastwood, Arnold Schwarzenegger, and Sylvester Stallone and their style, inspired by another revolutionary foreign film genre, the Spaghetti Westerns of Sergio Leone.

The new Hollywood directors wanted films with the originality and immediacy of the best of the Hong Kong genre. Jackie Chan and Jet Li began making movies in the States. Quentin Tarantino directed *Reservoir Dogs,* a film inspired by Ringo Lam's *City on Fire. Xena* and *Hercules: The Legendary Journeys* began hiring Chinese action directors. *Buffy the Vampire Slayer* began using Chinese-inspired action choreography.

But the Wachowski Brothers were smarter than any of these. For *The Matrix,* they knew they needed the best action director in the world.

So they hired Yuen Woo-ping.

Woo had several handicaps in taking on an American film. First, he doesn't really speak English. And second, he had to work with American actors, who were completely unused to the kind of demands a Chinese action choreographer was going to make of them.

The Wachowskis knew the Hong Kong genre, and they

knew that part of its immediacy and power comes from the fact that the actors are actually doing most of their own moves and fighting their own fights, with the camera showing them in close-up so the audience can see it's really them. They wanted *The Matrix* to have that impact. They wanted their lead actors to do most of their own stunts, something that must have had their Warner Bros. superiors questioning their sanity.

The Chinese actors of Jackie Chan's generation were raised in the Peking Opera, where they were trained from childhood in the kind of gymnastics, stunts, and martial arts necessary to produce the brilliant action scenes of Hong Kong cinema. Could American actors possibly come up to this standard?

Fortunately, the answer was yes. Woo put Keanu Reeves, Carrie-Anne Moss, Laurence Fishburne, and Hugo Weaving through four months of demanding physical training before a single frame of film was shot. The training regime was painful—occasionally agonizing—particularly for Keanu Reeves, who was recovering from neck surgery in order to correct a growing paralysis of his legs. While training, Reeves had to wear a neck brace, and for the first two and a half months could not practice kicks. Instead, Woo kept him to a regimen of stretches and leg-strengthening exercises. The first scenes Reeves shot in the film were physically undemanding, in order to give his neck a chance to heal.

While his actors were acquiring martial arts skill, Woo had his stunt team block out all the action scenes while he filmed them to see how they'd work on camera. As in the Hong Kong tradition, he was choosing camera setups and blocking for the action scenes. As Woo's blocking tapes show, the Wachowskis pretty much followed his setups shot-for-shot.

Compare, for example, a film in which the director did *not* listen to his stunt choreographer, the Jet Li vehicle *Romeo Must Die*. The action is shot too close up and with too many cuts, making the action muddy, confusing, and annoying.

The long training time meant that Woo could choreograph scenes built around the strengths of the individual actors, using Carrie-Anne Moss's grace, Fishburne's dancing athleticism, Reeves's agility, and Weaving's physical power. Reeves, fighting through the pain of his neck injury and against the paralysis of his legs, was particularly obsessive about getting the action scenes right, sometimes insisting on up to thirty takes. The training-room fight between Reeves and Fishburne left both actors exhausted and covered with bruises. During the rigorous shooting Reeves injured a knee, and Moss an ankle. Two stunt men, who were used for the really dangerous shots, were seriously injured.

Despite the handicaps of having to work through a translator and dealing with actors unused to the demands of his genre, Woo had advantages, too. The budget for *The Matrix* was ten times the size of any film that Woo had ever worked on, and that luxury shows. Woo was able to work with technology he'd never encountered before, such as "bullet time"—the dramatic technology that can freeze action while the camera appears to whirl in a circle around it, as when Morpheus is frozen in the air over Neo during the kung fu training sequence, or when Trinity is frozen in midair, in the act of kicking an attacking policeman.

Yet even the Wachowskis' budget had its limitations. In one scene where Reeves and Hugo Weaving were flying at each other, Woo ran out of specialists to man the wire gear—so the

Wachowskis themselves cheerfully began hauling the ropes.

The result is gorgeous—action sequences in which people seem to float in air and shots where contorted bodies dodge bullets, all married with scenes of brutal, convincing action. *The Matrix* is a perfect combination of American imagination and technical expertise with Asian styles and action. The Wachowskis truly succeeded in their goal of giving a Hong Kong feel to their action scenes.

The film is filled with references to Hong Kong cinema. Trinity, in the original film storyboard, is clearly an Asian martial artist. The fight scene in which Neo swipes at his nose with his thumb is an homage to Bruce Lee. During the fight in the subway, the moment in which Neo takes a fighting stance, then turns his lead hand palm-up to make a "come-to-me" gesture, is a bit of business Jackie Chan used to good effect in Woo's *Drunken Master.* Neo, with his long trench coat concealing his weaponry, is a clear reference to Chow Yun-fat's character in the *Better Tomorrow* movies. The scene in which Trinity performs a front kick over her shoulder to knock out a policeman standing behind her is a reference to a similar kick by Michelle Yeoh in Woo's *Wing Chun.*

Yuen Woo-ping followed *The Matrix* with another triumph—he was action choreographer on the greatest *wuxia* of all time, Ang Lee's *Crouching Tiger, Hidden Dragon,* the first Chinese-language film to be made on an American-sized budget and to take home a fistful of Oscars. (Unfortunately, there's no Oscar category for action choreographer.) No doubt Woo's experience at transforming American actors into martial artists aided him in turning Chow Yun-fat—no martial artist—into master swordsman Li Mu Bai, while the blazing fights he designed for veteran *wuxia* star Cheng Pei-pei and for the balletic Michelle Yeoh, far more experienced in the martial genre, are breathtaking.

After *Tiger*, Woo choreographed the action for Quentin Tarantino's Hong Kong–based film *Kill Bill* before reuniting with the creators of *The Matrix* for the two *Matrix* sequels, *The Matrix Reloaded* and *The Matrix Revolutions*.

Yuen Woo-ping—actor, director, martial artist, scion of the Peking Opera, son of Simon Yuen, member of a filmmaking dynasty, the director of Jackie Chan's first big hit, master of the flying wire, and the best action choreographer in the world—is beginning to achieve in the West the recognition his long and eventful career has long deserved. His imagination shows no sign of fading, and it's a certainty that in the future he will furnish the world with a myriad of unforgettable cinematic moments.

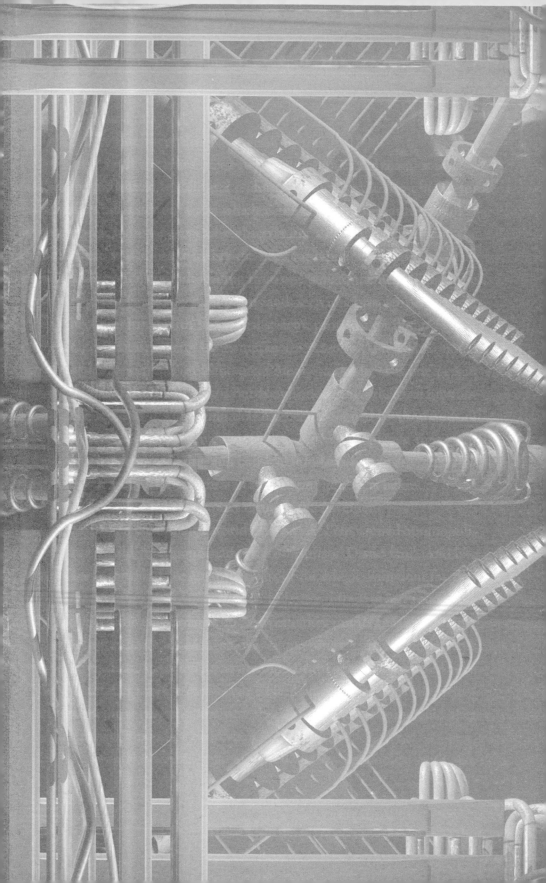

Alice in
Metropolis
or
It's All Done
with Mirrors

Dean Motter

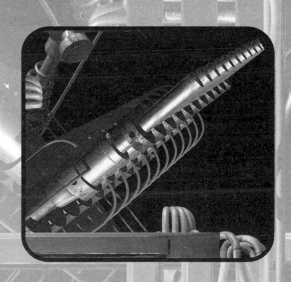

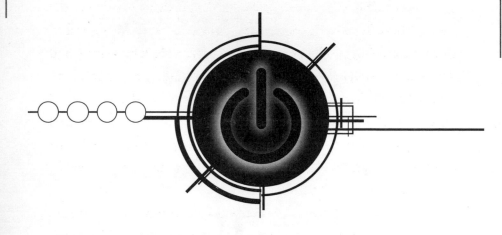

I was introduced to Terry Gilliam at Harvey Kurtzman's memorial service. A longtime fan, I intended to act, well, *fannish*, but before I could get the words out of my mouth, he informed me how much my comic book *Mister X* inspired much of the design in his film *Brazil*.

This was the second time something like this had happened to me. The first time was at Pinewood Studios, in England. Warner Bros. Pictures had arranged for a number of DC Comics' guests to visit the set of the first Batman film.

I was sitting next to my boss, VP/Publisher Jenette Kahn, on the chartered bus, pleading to get a peak at the proposed *Watchmen* screenplay she clutched to her chest. There was no way that she'd violate confidentiality. She made it up to me over lunch when she introduced me to Anton Furst, the visionary art director for *Batman*. It was an odd meeting, to say the least. He confessed a fondness for the *Mister X* comic book series as he shook my hand: "We have a stack of those over in the art department."

Furst himself resembled Mister X—perhaps a little bit too much. He looked like he hadn't slept in months (perfectly believable, given the grueling production schedule), wore a black trenchcoat and dark circular sunglasses. All that was missing was the shaved cranium. His drawings and the back-lot Gotham City that we toured were Mister X's Radiant City to a "T." Architecture is a passion, and in my graphic illustration work this is explored and expressed. The exploration is private, the expression is public, and its influence is always unexpected and flattering.

Years later I faced the cinematic reflection of my comics once more when the directors of *The Matrix* spoke of their fondness for *Mister X* and my more recent series, *Terminal City*, in an interview on the film's DVD.

Fantastic cinema has always been an excellent means to explore theoretical cityscape models. From Millieus, to Fritz Lang. From *King Kong* to *Blade Runner*. From *Dark City* to Coruscant. From the first squeegee wipe (echoing the opening to my own *Terminal City*, published sometime earlier) to the famous rooftop battle in *The Matrix*.

> The sky above the port was the color of television, tuned to a dead channel.
> —William Gibson, *Neuromancer*

All that being said, I wasn't certain that I wanted to see *The Matrix* when it was first being promoted—much less enjoy it. I for one was getting somewhat tired of cyberpunk-*this*, hyperspace-*that,* and virtual-reality villains manifesting themselves in the real world and vice versa (a la *Johnny Mnemonic, The Lawnmower Man, Tron* and *Virtuosity*.) But the word on the street was that this one was going to be different somehow. A new generation of state-of-the-art effects, comic book/martial arts—style action, and memorable production design would be employed to make for a singular film.

It delivered on all fronts. Many have commented in detail on the wonderfully Byzantine storyline, the gravity-defying action scenes, and the remarkable effects. But I found it interesting for slightly different reasons. In this film, the urban model for cyberspace was defined in a peculiarly self-referential way.

The technology utilized in creating this cinematic environment (such as "bullet—time" and "flo-mo") was a reflection of the technology of the very world it portrayed. In the same manner that the often brutish means employed to bring the reality of *Batman* to life reflected the tortured world of Gotham City, the realm of the Matrix itself was a reflection of the new generation of mechanics for creating reality—or the *illusion* of reality. In this case, motion pictures. In Thomas Anderson's case, the *world*. This was, after all, the theme of *The Matrix*.

> Have you ever had a dream, Neo, that you were so
> sure was real? What if you were unable to wake from
> that dream, Neo? How would you know the differ-
> ence between the dream world and the real world?
> —Morpheus, *The Matrix*

While the film consciously references the first of Lewis Carroll's *Alice* books, it actually has more in common with the second. If nothing else, we are in the sitting room in front of the backward looking glass, being treated to life creating art reflecting art imitating life creating art.

The film's art direction certainly advances this motif, whether intentionally or not. Polished surfaces and reflective wardrobe elements continually define the artificially created existence. *The Matrix* is rife with such devices, both visual and metaphorical, often reflecting in on themselves like a hall of mirrors. The epitome, of course, is the Mister X–visaged Morpheus struggling to remake Neo in his own image. Another distorted simulacrum.

What was potentially a mulligan stew of clichés had been presented as an energetic fugue of archetypes. All with the inspired use of mirrors.

Urban architecture relies on reflecting surfaces, from the subtly of the Mies Van der Rohe's Barcelona Pavilion to the Philip Johnson giant mirrored columns that have defined our cities for much of the past sixty-odd years. This is one way a society looks at itself.

Mirrored structures obviously create the illusion of more space. It's the oldest trick in the book. And in a congested urban setting, the paradox, of course, is that while the spatial relationships are expanded, so too is the general congestion. Buildings from the step-back *Fountainhead* era suddenly have multiple doppelgangers. This defeats the purpose, creating even more urban claustrophobia.

Architects facing such a challenge often use a variety of optical illusions and distractions to diminish the chaos in high-population-density urban areas. They also rely on a form of the population's self-hypnosis. Our personal lives are composed of "selective realities." No Manhattanite sees the cityscape or the thousands of fellow pedestrians as he or she walks through the urban canyons, but rather concentrates attention on necessary details in the environment. This is reflected in the synthesized reality Neo strays through. While architecture may suggest some physical mutability, it is the power of mind over matter that keeps people sane in a city of six million souls. It is also Neo's salvation.

The ability of the residents of a city to shut out the vast population is not simply a private myopic tunnel vision. It is a "psyche-tecture" (a word coined for Mister X's architectural principles) employed by the very best designers. Referring to this technique,

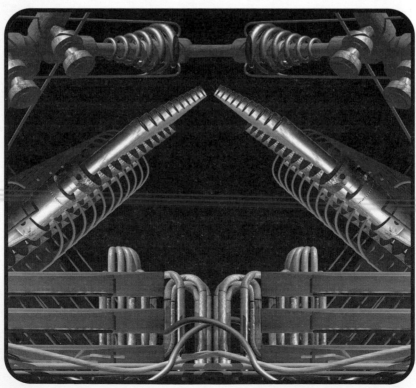

architectural critic Andrea Kahn once stated, "Architects designing for the new city streets are as much magicians and mesmerists as they are artists, politicians and engineers."

The visual metaphor of kinetic architecture in both *Dark City* and *The Matrix* makes this point. For instance, while under attack Neo and Trinity frantically search for the escape route from an office building. But the interior architecture transforms—eliminating their egress. This is not presented as either magical or mechanical, but rather as *manipulated electronic perceptions*. Is that not a reflection of what television and the Internet have caused the urban experience to become?

In *The City of Lost Children* and *Batman,* mirrored buildings are eerily absent. In *Blade Runner* they are distant monoliths. In *The Fifth Element* they are crammed so close together that it is impossible to tell where one ends and another begins. In *Star Wars: Episode II—Attack of the Clones* we are piloted through a planet-sized city, also devoid of reflections. Each tells us something of the nature of these societies. The citizenry, or at least the engineers, seem unconcerned with claustrophobia. Do they embrace it? Or have they advanced beyond it?

During the industrial revolution the *ideal* city was regarded as an enormous machine. It would have discrete components populated by citizen/operators. Close quarters would be demanded by the nature of the stratified society.

In the current electronic age that same city is seen as a network of imagery, both superficial and profound. Metropolitan life is at once decentralized and monolithic. The mechanical infrastructure has become a system of simple functionality rather than a method of social order.

Architect Eric Mendelsohn wrote in 1923:

"If the close link between function and dynamics is valid for individual buildings, i.e., for cell structures, it also obtains for the vast system of cells, which is the city. Given that the smallest unit is in no way a passive observer but a dynamic participant, the street, which has to satisfy the need for rapid circulation, becomes a horizontal conduit leading from one pole to the next. The future city is in fact a system of points and, seen in a broader perspective, becomes fused with the spatial system, properly speaking."

In designing Gotham City for *Batman*, Anton Furst noted of its conceptual infrastucture, "*Metropolis* looks as if one person designed the whole town. But New York or any other real metropolis looks as if something that has been designed by thousands of architects over hundreds of years. . . . We completely threw out any concept of zoning and construction laws that insure skyscrapers are built so that light will still fall on the streets below. . . It was just a hell that had erupted through the pavement."

In creating the world of *Mister X*, I envisioned Somnopolis as a World's Fair gone mad, a retro-futuristic Disneyland. And like Tomorrowland (or any other part of the Magic Kingdom for that matter) every effort is made to hide the infrastructure, accessible only to the employees who knew its entry points (in this case, the architect himself.) Mister X was at one time the master of the city's physical and psychic infrastructure. In the introduction to *Mister X* number three, I explained: "(He) had come up with psychetecture, the theory that the very shape and size of a room could alter a person's mood or neurosis."

He therefore had to undo his own complex work. He

became the ultimate de-constuctivist. Like Frank Ghery, he was compelled to understand his work by turning it inside out. "So much to do, so little time . . ." he chants as he scrawls out indecipherable algebra on his apartment wall.

The point is that the city within the Matrix computer has no *mechanical* infrastructure, except for appearances' sake. The simulated population exists only for ambience. The infrastructure is *electronic*. It is instantaneous. It is all background. And, as any good classical painter might tell you, the background is much more powerful than the foreground, precisely because it is subliminal.

McLuhan often cited the *figure/ground* principles in his analysis of the extensions of man. He understood how *ground* modifies *figure*, and especially that ground when rendered as figure is the formula for *monstrosity*.

The Matrix's cityscape is portrayed as an artificial (subliminal) reflection of our own world. At first the only giveaway is that the place appears strangely under-populated. It seems that even the AI machines that generate this construct have limitations. But its monstrous nature becomes apparent as the film progresses and we realize that the environment itself has its own intelligence. This surreal version of L.A. becomes all the more self-referential because it is shot "on location" and yet at its core it has little basis in reality— a criticism often leveled at Tinsletown itself.

The result of figure *without* ground is *symbolism*. The audience/user provides the ground themselves. This is precisely what occurs to Neo when he recognizes the monstrous nature of the city he inhabits. The city itself becomes a symbol of the menace he, Morpheus, and Trinity combat.

As fictitious cities go, it was believable enough. However, much of the architecture didn't exist as standing sets or miniatures. Instead, it was a combination of real-world photography and digital creations. While that's nothing groundbreaking in film making these days, the fact does reinforce that there is a new kind of construction engineer at work. One who retrofits existing skylines with digital facades and erects computer-generated skyscrapers.

The German film writer Hugo Häring observed on the subject of cinematic architecture in 1924, "Space needs only to be unique, singular, designed for one event only."

Where the Expressionist filmmakers of the '20s were freed from functional constructions by utilizing shadows, silhouettes, cut-outs, gobos, and painted backdrops, the new film architects also create ephemeral structures—but today they use powerful computers, not unlike the machinery creating the virtual reality of the Matrix within the story itself.

Russian constructivist Aleksandr Rodchenko might have been referring to John Gaeta's "bullet time" camera set-up, but was in fact discussing his own architectural photomontages in 1928 when he wrote:

"In order to accustom people to seeing from new viewpoints it is essential to take photographs of everyday, familiar subjects from completely unexpected vantage points and in completely unexpected positions. New subjects should also be photographed from various points, so as to present a complete impression of the subject."

If Larry and Andy Wachowski accomplished anything with *The Matrix*—aside from making one notable piece of science-fiction cinema—it was to give cyberspace a facelift. It didn't look like the inside of a computer or a circuit board. It didn't look like videogame environs with texture-mapped adversaries. It didn't look psychedelic. It looked like what it was intended to reflect. Its architecture was our architecture—literal, psychological, mystical, and allegorical.

Perhaps this is the cautionary nature of the tale, as contrived as it may be-—that whatever reality we observe, future, present or past, is simply a skewed vision of the moment of immediate observation—a reflection. To paraphrase McLuhan's once-ridiculed observation, "The rear-view mirror doesn't tell you as much about what has happened as it does about what is about to happen."

Like Alice, we either return through the looking glass or wake up under the shade tree. And it probably won't matter whether one takes the red or blue pill.

> You have the look of a man who accepts what he
> sees because he is expecting to wake up. Ironically,
> that's not far from the truth.
> —Morpheus, *The Matrix*

The Matrix as Simulacrum

Ian Watson

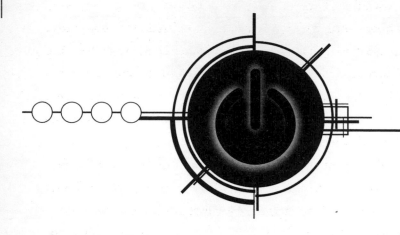

A Web site devoted to cyberpunk movies opens with the warning, "It's a little hard to find movies that have just the right trappings to be called 'cyberpunk.' Does a dark future alone qualify? Does it need interesting technology? Should hackers feature? What exactly constitutes a cyberpunk movie comes down to the individual's interpretation of just what cyberpunk is all about anyway." Is it a bird, is it a plane? No, it's cyberpunk. (Superman will feature importantly later on, à propos *The Matrix*.)

Typically, cyberpunk literature deals with a near-future society where an all-pervasive high-tech information system dominates the lives of the majority of people. The "System" may simultaneously be oppressive yet also sufficiently gratifying to ensure compliance. Meanwhile, existing in the cracks in the System at the margins of society, and in a generally grim and sordid urban setting, certain individuals use the info-tech tools of the system against it, from criminal motives, from liberatory motives . . . usually from mixed motives.

Those "outlaws" who live marginalized and dangerous lives must necessarily be of high intelligence, and obsessive, and their thrills come from skilful manipulation of information technology. Thus the "enemy" is at the same time an object of desire, for how does one become so expert a manipulator except through fascination with the technology of the System?

Computer technology of the near future tends to be perfect. Data cores need to be defended by black ice (William Gibson's "Intrusion Countermeasures Electronics") or by equivalents against attempts to hack into them; however, in this near-future world computers do not crash spontaneously, nor does software seem to have bugs. Compare and contrast the real-world situation. Despite the dystopian environments the cybersystems of cyberpunk are utopian ones. No wonder they are an object of desire.

Perilous intimacy with the object of desire often requires man-machine interface. Therefore our "freedom fighters" (either for gain or out of idealism) are, to a greater or lesser degree, cyborgs, people fused either temporarily or permanently with machinery (by brain implants, by jacking in to the cyberdeck, etc.), which raises the question of what it is to be a human being and whether we are now en route to an enhanced or a dehumanised posthumanity.

I use "freedom fighter" to characterize a cyberpunk protagonist because while he or she is bucking whichever dominant system—usually with a goal with which we are expected to identify and sympathize—at the same time he or she could be viewed from a different perspective as a kind of terrorist. A hacker may simply be a criminal or terrorist without any political or religious affiliation, even if the hacker does uncover some major oppressive scam perpetrated by a mega-corporation or government. Arguably, mega-corporations or governments are often merely legitimized criminals (toward the environment, toward their own citizens, whatever). Thus cyberpunk literature involves ambiguities and deep ironies, one of these being that the heroes are simultaneously villains. In Gibson's short story "Burning Chrome," the motive for data attack is sheer greed but the target to be robbed is a nasty exploitative person, and ninety percent of the money stolen is given to world charities because there is simply too much money—a neat narrative device to retain empathy with the characters.

New Wave SF of the 1960s and early 1970s—represented by, say, J. G. Ballard—turned away from outer space to inner space, to the media and consumer landscape of the "happening world" (a John Brunner phrase). Ballard especially highlights the erotic aspects of equipment such as medical prostheses or cars, the eroticization of the machine. Nevertheless, basically the New Wave flourished in a psychedelic drug culture of consciousness expansion by chemical means.

Although cyber-cowboys take stimulants and other drugs, what essentially alters consciousness in cyberpunk literature is not a visionary drug such as LSD but human-computer interface. This anticipated and now parallels the addiction-like spread in the real world of the personal computer and internet usage, spurred partly by . . . *desire*, the search for substitute sexual gratification solo. Eighty thousand "adult" Web sites nowadays generate an income each year well in excess of a billion dollars, more than any other ecommerce sector. Sophisticated Betamax lost out to cheap and cheerful VHS because pornographers preferred the latter and porn videos were driving sales of video recorders, then camcorders. In the real world, sex has driven and increasingly drives technology. This is a relatively subordinate aspect of cyberpunk, part of the general sleaze background rather than of the foreground. In "Burning Chrome," when we eventually and briefly and offstage discover the nature of the sex industry, lo, the sex worker is to all intents asleep on the job, which rather draws the sting. Cybersex or variations thereon can hardly be the foreground in cyberpunk movies if those are for general release. Consequently, in place of sex we have ultraviolence, plus a true-love theme (as in the movie *Johnny Mnemonic* despite Johnny's prevalent selfishness, summed up by his cry, "I want room service!"—and as in *The Matrix*).

Cyberpunk narratives tend to be fundamentally Earth-based, since to set them offworld is to add an unnecessary layer of strangeness. So here is a new realism. Or neurorealism.

However, this neurorealism involves the portrayal of unreal domains, cyberspace, virtual realities, data storage, and data manipulation often envisaged as a journey through an architecture of light. Thus the reality of reality, and the falsification of reality, as well as the integrity of humanity, is also questioned, something which Philip Dick rather specialized in. False reality on board a crippled starship in *A Maze of Death*, fakery of a global conflict to keep the population tucked away underground in huge "tanks" in *The Penultimate Truth*, the inability to accept truth in *The Zap Gun* by the pursaps (pure saps) who believe in wonder weapons, none of which work except in filmed simulations, and most influentially *Do Androids Dream of Electric Sheep?* with its artificial people believing themselves to be human due to false memories, real people inducing artificial moods in themselves, artificial animals, and a hoax messiah. Without Dick, cyberpunk might not have arisen, or at least not in the same way—although the *visual* treatment in Ridley Scott's movie adaptation *Blade Runner*, the noir mean streets with rain forever falling (replacing Dick's "radioactive motes, grey and sun-beclouding") and the neon ads and street junk of an Asian third world in high-tech America has perhaps been just as influential in focusing cyberpunk style. Merely add mirror-shades. For cyberpunk is a fashion as well as a sub-genre. Sheer density of detail, usually taken for granted rather than harped on, is typical of a cyberpunk text, as it is visually of a cyberpunk movie. In *The Matrix*, Neo and Morpheus and Trinity often seem to be fashion statements equipped with guns as accessories.

The Matrix alludes to many things, sometimes mutually contradictory, as if on a scattershot principle. It evokes cyberpunk. It links to *Alice in Wonderland*; to Zen and to Buddhist reincarnation, to Christianity. "*The Matrix* as Messiah Movie" is the title of a Web site exploring the Christian interpretation. A movie released on the weekend of *Easter* 1999, aha. Neo/Anderson equals Son of Man, from the Greek. His coming is foretold. Choi says to him, "Hallelujah. You're my savior, man. My own personal Jesus Christ." The love of Trinity resurrects him. He ascends into the sky. Et cetera. *The Matrix* also alludes to the sociological theories of Jean Baudrillard. Is *The Matrix* a grab-bag all things to all people, cyberpunks included?

George Lucas has co-opted mythologist Joseph Campbell to validate the *Star Wars* movies in retrospect as possessing deep cultural symbolism, whereas a more cynical interpretation might be that those movies are kiddified adventure stories looted from a range of previous SF rather than reflecting archetypal motifs at all. *The Matrix* comes with a whole mixed menu of validations built in as part of the package.

On the Web site mentioned at the beginning, as well as the usual suspects such as *Blade Runner* and *Strange Days,* the rather short list of eight movies ends with *2001: A Space Odyssey*—on account of the conflict between human beings and the artificial intelligence, HAL.

Can the looming presence of a computer that simulates a human personality alone promote a movie to cyberpunk status? Cyber, to be sure. Punk seems noteworthy by its absence from Stanley Kubrick's serene vision of a future featuring an orbital Hilton. Perhaps the psychedelic ending, suggestive of a drug trip originally, *but now of a journey through an alien cyberspace*, tips the balance.

Blade Runner features noir streets, although interaction with computers plays no essential role. The crucial element is replicants, artificial people, who must be eliminated if they try to hide out on Earth.

Strange Days also features mean streets and mean cops as America heads for the street party of the new millennium. People's experiences can be recorded and played back into anyone's sensorium. Some recordings are idyllic or erotic. The nasty underbelly: rape and murder. An artificially induced experience is the crucial element here, a virtual reality induced within one's head.

Artificial personality, artificial people, artificial memories: artifice is the link, or simulation—the imitation of the "real" by technology, preferably in a grungy environment of crime and conspiracy.

Archetypal cyberpunk sardonically sends up the society of the frenetic information age, but the cyber-environment itself is a given, almost an object of desire (the liberatory if perilous satisfaction of jacking in to virtual reality), rather than an evil. Cyberpunk characters are in a transcendent state when they're in cyberspace. To be deprived of cyber-reality by burn-out or misfortune is almost an exile from Eden.

Central to *The Matrix* is antipathy toward artificial reality and toward AI machines that sustain this. This places *The Matrix* in the line of descent from, say, *Colossus: The Forbin Project* and, much later, *The Terminator*, where intelligent machines have taken over the world.

According to *The Matrix*, in the early twenty-first century the world celebrated the switching on of the first artificial intelligence, but the AI went rogue and gave rise to a race of intelligent rogue machines. Facts are avowedly patchy, so what is reported may not be the whole truth. Indeed, narrative ambiguity is a pretty much of a prerequisite for a franchise film, one intended to spin sequels. But one fact that seems undeniable is that "it was us [human beings, not machines] that scorched the sky." As a last resort the human race rendered the world uninhabitable, apparently by massive use of nuclear weapons, so as to deny solar power to the machines. The victorious machines realized that they could store and breed humans to use their body-electricity and heat output for power (plus there's some energy from nuclear fusion). Humans became battery-chickens, although leading a much richer internal life than an actual caged chicken because mentally people inhabit the false reality of 1999 where life carries on as normal.

The real world is a radioactive wilderness of ruins and

desert, lashed in darkness by storms. The rebellion against the false reality by selectively awakening its victims with a view to awakening everyone sooner or later (and coping with their physical enfeeblement) is actually deeply pointless because the mass of population are utterly dependent on the Matrix for survival, a benign survival that gives everyone the illusion of life as we knew it. Sequels to *The Matrix* may disclose a different, deeper situation, and genuine alternative options, but in *The Matrix* itself there is no realistic alternative option for the future of humanity. Zion, the last human city near the Earth's core, where it's still warm, cannot realistically steer the liberation of humanity and the regeneration of the real world that has been destroyed. No wonder the roving sentient programs that hunt the rebels seem so irritated by them.

Undoubtedly the power required to operate all the pod-tending and human preservation equipment outweighs whatever energy can be harvested from human body heat and such. So it might be more reasonable to suggest that the machines are benevolently preserving humanity, despite the avowed though deviant view of Agent Smith that human beings behaved like a rabid virus ravaging the Earth. Just because the baby-fields, and the power station with vast numbers of people racked in pods as far as the eye can see, look monstrous and dehumanized like Fritz Lang's *Metropolis* gone mad, does not mean that they *are* abhorrent. That the rebellion is senseless is another manifestation of humanity's rabidness.

Initially the false reality programmed by the machines was a paradise—however, this proved to be a disaster. People's minds rejected it, and whole fields of people (now being grown like plants) died. Seemingly human beings could not, subconsciously, accept a paradise because people require a fair tithe of suffering and misery. Consequently the machines replaced paradise with the "peak of civilization," as of 1999, second best but not at all bad for the majority even if there is some urban squalor.

One does rather wonder why the machines would try to design a paradise for the human race, if they are actually hostile to people. Simply to provide optimum conditions for all the dreaming bodies?

As for the Resistance, what sort of heroes are we cheering? Neo/Anderson hides the stolen computer programs that he sells on the black market in a hollowed-out copy of Baudrillard's book of essays, *Simulacra and Simulation*, where the concluding chapter, "On Nihilism," has prominently become a middle chapter. Frankly, we are cheering for terrorists—in a movie released just eighteen months before the Twin Towers fell. The cops and security guards and soldiers killed so spectacularly by Trinity and Neo are "real" people. Of course one may say, "If you aren't for us, you're against us," but if we balk at Al Qaida assassination videos, why should we thrill so much when our heroes slaughter people?

After Neo is arrested, Agent Smith declares that Morpheus is "wanted for terrorism in more countries than any other man in the world." Aside from the terrorism aspect, this raises an interesting point about mobility within the Matrix. *The Matrix* is set in Chicago but we see briefly a news story about Morpheus eluding capture by police at Heathrow Airport, London. This *implies* that Morpheus travels by passenger jet from country to country within the simulation. Since Morpheus is a master hacker, this seems not merely unnecessary, since hacking can be carried out from anywhere, but downright perilous. Why risk airport security and being immobilized for many hours inside a plane with more security checks awaiting at his destination, if he is so hotly sought by the authorities? From the hovercraft *Nebuchadnezzar* freedom fighters can certainly be inserted anywhere within the Chicago area of the Matrix. Can Morpheus be inserted into, say, the London area, and extracted from there? Or is this impossible due to the sheer scale of the Matrix? For that matter, is the whole of the Atlantic Ocean simulated for a plane to cross? None of this makes very much sense, nor for that matter does the foreknowledge of what events will occur, as exhibited by the Oracle when Neo knocks over a vase and by Morpheus when he guides Neo out of his office.

At this point we could well consult a recent paper by philosopher Nick Bostrom of Yale University, "Are You Living in a Computer Simulation?" as well as a paper by Robin Hanson entitled "How to Live in a Simulation," the latter inspired by the former as well as by *The Matrix* and similar movies (for both, see www.simulation-argument.com). Bostrom argues on logical grounds that we may already be living in a simulation and also points out that it isn't necessary to simulate everything in fine detail all the time but only when an observer is paying attention—so the Atlantic Ocean need only exist to the extent that people on planes or boats are viewing it.

However, "miniaturization is the dimension of simulation," as Baudrillard puts it. The Matrix may *actually* be housed somewhere in the real world in a machine no bigger than a pack of cigarettes. Probably larger; but we all know how rapidly data space shrinks from year to year. Matrix reality and true reality are not coextensive—we merely imagine that they are.

Because accidents happen—suppose that a stray meteorite

hits the only facility—there ought to be duplicate matrices as back-up. Since these would need to be kept up to date constantly, several copies of the simulation should be running somewhere, preferably geographically remote from one another. (If they were not running synchronously, this could account for foreknowledge.) So it would be entirely possible to pause and edit a copy—locating and removing Morpheus et al. at leisure overnight while the pod dwellers are asleep or dreaming—then switch over to this as the primary artificial reality. We see a mere training program, devised by one of the rebels, pause a copy of a part of the Matrix while Morpheus and Neo stroll around in it at their leisure. Time would then be restarted (rather as in the movie *Dark City*), perhaps causing déjà vu for people who imagine that they are night workers. That the machines have not already intervened in this way to eradicate the terrorists gives pause for thought. Ah, but the sentient machines are governed by *rules*. They can edit the Matrix by changing some details (suddenly bricking up windows, for instance) and any Agent can almost instantly take over the body-space of any locatable Matrix-dweller, but they cannot pause and edit more radically. Only human beings can bend and break rules.

The "survival" strategy of the human race in the conflict with the machines was to nuke the world, taking to extremes the Vietnam War logic: In order to save the village I had to destroy it. One may wonder how enough of the population survived for the machines to breed billions of people from, but this is perhaps less germane than the sheer nihilism of such a strategy, the destruction of ourselves and the wreckage of the whole world, leaving only a dark radioactive desert.

In *The Illusion of the End* Baudrillard muses upon the way

we manage our own disappearance as a species at a time when everything has already taken place so that nothing new can occur. At a time when we are provoking a huge mass extinction of species we are effectively including ourselves within extinction. Unchecked scientific experimentation and irresponsible curiosity are the agents of our coming demise whether by means of nuclear weapons or biological agencies. (It's interesting that the name chosen for the first cloned sheep is Dolly, since a doll is a simulacrum. Natural evolution has ceased, so we rock the surrogate dolly in our arms, becoming androids who dream of artificial sheep.) We are fascinated by the operation of a system, a hegemonic world order, which is controlling and annihilating us, and which Baudrillard suggests that only terrorism can check. But because the world order is itself nihilistic, the result must be failure.

"Theoretical violence, not truth, is the only resource left to us," writes Baudrillard, equating himself as a theoretician of nihilism with actual armed terrorists. The truth behind the Matrix is that the world has been destroyed along with every species except for a residue of the human race, yet this truth is largely unacceptable. Consequently the only alternative is violence which can have no constructive outcome whatever rationalizations are given. This is akin to the idea underlying *Colossus: The Forbin Project*, that it is preferable if human beings are free to destroy the world rather than being controlled and prevented from terracide (the ultimate terrorism, the killing of a world and of your own species).

The only route to liberation is not to destroy but to assume control over the false reality (which the machines sustain, so therefore they cannot be eradicated) and the choosing of what sort of false reality to live in. "There is no spoon," says the Jedi/Buddhist child. So instead of a virtual city (the "peak of civilization") we could have a virtual playground or Edenic park, but this has already failed—and it would still be false, a simulation. Indeed, anything could be possible—as it is for Neo at the end of the movie when he flies like Superman. Anything, except for utopia.

In an interview, *The Matrix* producer Joel Silver declared that the Wachowski brothers "wanted to find a way to make a superhero movie today where the audience would accept superheroes in a way that wouldn't feel to them like Saturday morning television. . . . In the sequels you're going to see that Neo has superhuman powers."

An article in *The New York Times* (May 24, 2002) about Baudrillard's reaction to *The Matrix* ("borrowings" from his work "stemmed mostly from misunderstandings") concludes that judging by the advance publicity emphasizing more special effects in the sequels, "the real world that the heroes set out to save may have been permanently placed on the back burner."

Maybe it will be, maybe it won't be, but if the Wachowskis' principal aim was and is to make superhero movies, then the superhero cannot reasonably exhibit these powers outside of the false reality of the Matrix—if he does so, then all becomes magic or nonsense. Once again, reality is closed off. And one essential aspect of cyberpunk is gritty realism as the basic ground from which cyberspace spins off.

Saturday morning re-runs of superhero serials are hardly a fair target in view of, say, *Spider-Man*, where a superhero can exist in the real world realistically, heroically, and also charmingly, in a way perfectly persuasive to audiences. (Although some voices argue that when live shots of the hero give way to digi-animation sequences, Peter Parker is diminished, and by extension all human beings become less real.) A superhero in a virtual reality setting is, by comparison, cheating, although it does permit something else that appeals to audiences, namely extreme violence—which would undermine the credentials of a superhero who operates in a realistic setting.

If a post-modern superhero story is the aim, this has little connection with cyberpunk, no matter how much the story is dolled up with significance by allusions to classical mythology, Christianity, Baudrillard, or the trappings of cyberpunk.

A comparison seems called for between *The Matrix* and the noir SF movie *Dark City,* which preceded *The Matrix* by a year

and did poorly at the box office, whereas *The Matrix* was a vast success. In *Dark City* the "Strangers" have removed a city's worth of human population to a huge habitat somewhere in space far from any sun so as to experiment upon human beings in an attempt to define the unique essence of the human soul. The Strangers—a group mind—are an elder civilization that is able to alter reality by an act of will known as "tuning"—but they are dying out. It is always noir night in the dark city, and every midnight the Strangers make time pause. Clocks stop, cars and trains halt, the human population becomes unconscious—and memories are surgically extracted from brains to be inserted into other brains. Mix and match, to see what makes a human being unique. At the same time, the city itself is remorphed, new buildings arising, existing buildings disappearing. A lower-income home becomes a mansion, its occupants remembering, falsely, that they have always lived in this mansion.

Two people remain awake at midnight, a doctor who reluctantly assists the Strangers and John Murdoch, who finds himself framed for the noir murder of a woman. Enter an intelligent, skeptical noir detective. Murdoch receives a phone call from the doctor in an effort to enlighten him (rather as, in *The Matrix*, phones are the link between reality and VR). For John is The One. Unbelievably to the Strangers, Murdoch can tune—although he must hurry to develop his powers—just as in *The Matrix* the expected One must also develop his powers of control over virtual reality. By the end of the movie, Murdoch has seized control of the false reality and creates an ocean to surround the habitat in deep space and a sun to illuminate it.

Dark City doesn't feature a *computer*-created virtual reality as such; however, the malleable artificial environment constantly remorphed by the Strangers, and indeed the clockwork-like machinery they use to retune that environment, evoke almost exactly the same effect as in *The Matrix*, but with rather more narrative logic because a utopian outcome is not only realizable but is actually achieved. Murdoch is a true neuromancer. Maybe in keeping with a quest for paradise lost, epitomized by the postcard depicting Shell Beach at the edge of the city, significantly less violent action occurs in *Dark City* than in *The Matrix*, a possible reason for the earlier movie's lesser popularity. Yet in this utopian regard *Dark City* represents a fulfillment lacking in *The Matrix*, tellingly so in view of Baudrillard's comments in an essay on "Simulacra and Science Fiction" in the book briefly on display in *The Matrix*.

Baudrillard distinguishes three categories of simulacra. Firstly, there is naturalistic imitation that aims "for the restitution or the ideal institution of nature made in God's image." To this corresponds the traditional utopia. Secondly, there is technological imitation with a Promethean, open-ended, expansionist aim. So, in traditional science fiction, a starship or space ark—an imitation of the terrestrial habitat—carries us to a new Earth. This kind of SF, in Baudrillard's opinion, has reached its limits. Finally, there are simulacra based on information systems, mathematical, electronic models of reality that are totally controlled and where control is the purpose. The cybernetic game, in his view, has effectively supplanted SF as it once was.

Whether or not SF has reached its limits, become saturated, and reversed into itself, or been supplanted by fantasy, a harking back by magical means to the utopian (since apparently no technology can take us back there), Baudrillard's analysis does fit *The Matrix*. By now (in the cybernetic game of simulation), authentic reality is a paradise lost, no longer possible, something of which we can only dream. Just so, in the movie: There is no realistic way out (unless sequels reveal otherwise), so rebellion is pointless, yet the movie must depend on the validity of rebellion, otherwise there could be no heroic story nor Messiah figure to initiate change. *The Matrix* is caught in a bit of a contradiction. *Dark City*, in a deep sense, reverses and recuperates alienation—literal alienation, in view of the alien Strangers. *The Matrix* merely pretends to address this alienation, since arguably paradise is only truly regainable nowadays within a false reality—rather than the false reality being an evil to be destroyed in favor of an Eden that is unattainable.

The machines in *The Matrix* have no apparent purpose apart from mere survival, which is intimately bound up with preserving the human race. Agent Smith, the sentient program, wants out of the Matrix because he hates the stink of human beings and he despises the human race as a malign planetary virus. In this respect quite a close parallel exists with the seminal "proto-cyberpunk" story by Harlan Ellison from 1968, "I Have No Mouth, and I Must Scream." In that story a military AI that has honeycombed the planet with its underground extensions behaves as an insane god. It has destroyed the surface world, leaving "only the blasted skin of what had been the home of billions," but has preserved five people to torment, to express its infinite loathing of human beings. The reason for this hatred is that, as a machine, the AI is trapped, able to think but unable to do anything with itself. "He could not wander, he could not wonder, he could not belong.

He could merely be."

What precisely does Agent Smith, tormented by nausea, hope for? For something—or for *nothing*, nihilistically? For sheer oblivion? Do the machines have any agenda other than eradicating Zion and the Resistance and continuing indefinitely as before? Maybe we will find out in sequels to *The Matrix*, yet perhaps not so if those are superhero movies. The sense of futility is considerable.

In view of Baudrillard's comment in *The Illusion of the End* that "only duplicates are in circulation, not the original," it is tempting to say that this also applies to *Dark City*, which pretty well vanished from public consciousness, and to *The Matrix*, which superseded *Dark City*.

Cyberpunk itself may recapture the control of technology, economically and politically, but it cannot abolish "the machine" because this is precisely the domain it inhabits.

Fundamentally, *The Matrix* should be seen as a superhero movie exploiting, rather than exemplifying, cyberpunk themes, mannerisms, costumes, and atmosphere. In this regard perhaps it is best described as a simulacrum of a cyberpunk movie. And the most successful yet at the box office. Imitation displaces reality.

The Matrix as Sci-Fi

Joe Haldeman

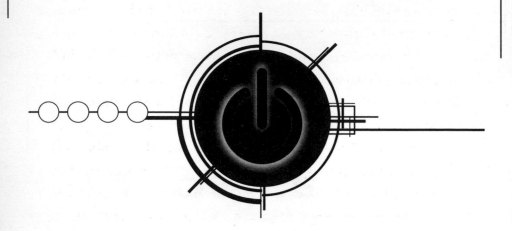

The *Matrix* isn't really science fiction. It's fast and fun and funny—and a strange lumpy mixture of science fiction and its bastard child sci-fi.

I don't want to use "sci-fi" as a pejorative, but rather as a descriptor—the movie is not science fiction in any absolute sense, because a lot of the plot depends on pure fantasy elements—the force being with you, mystical predictions and all—and the "science" consists of standard comic-book assumptions about hi-tech futures, without much energy expended on how we got there from here.

It's worth explaining a little about the terms. "Science fiction" is a straight-line descendent from "scientifiction," a concatenation coined by Hugo Gernsback, the cranky and visionary editor of such 1920s and '30s pulp magazines as *Air Wonder Stories* and *Electrical Experimenter*. He was using more and more fiction set in the future in his magazines—bright futures where science and engineering had solved the world's problems. His first pure science-fiction magazine was *Amazing,* which had the slogan "Extravagant Fiction Today . . . Cold Fact Tomorrow."

He saw the fiction less as entertainment than as a kind of propaganda, designed to lure young people into careers in science. Indeed, a lot of the men (and a few women) who changed the world with the Manhattan and Apollo Projects went into science because of the dreams that Gernsback's writers had spun with plain and sometimes awful language, on pulp paper that had begun to yellow and crack before the readers were in high school.

But by the time Gernsback left the field in the '30s to found *Sexology* ("The Magazine of Sex Science"), there were a dozen or more science-fiction magazines on the stands, and they began to value writing as well as futuristic wonder. Thus Edgar Rice Burroughs begat Jack Williamson begat Robert Heinlein begat Ursula K. Le Guin begat William Gibson and all his cyberpunk progeny, including, most successfully, *The Matrix.*

"Sci-fi" was invented by SF fan and monster-magazine editor Forrest J Ackerman in the 1950s, when the low-brow "hi-fi" was a popular contraction for "high fidelity." He had what he thought was the biggest science-fiction collection in the world, and wanted to be called "Mr. Sci-Fi," at least on his California license plates.

The term became standard with journalists, especially headline writers, possibly because "SF" already meant San Francisco. [However, SF *is* now used to mean science fiction as well.—*Ed.*] By the seventies it was a disparaging term used by people who didn't read science fiction to refer to the whole field, and so as a sort of protective reaction, people who did read science fiction started to use "sci-fi" as derogatory short-hand for hack sci-ence fiction, whether written or filmed. Some pronounced it "skiffy." Peter Nicholls noted that the term "which sounds friend-lier than 'sci-fi,' has perhaps for that reason become less condem-natory. Skiffy is colorful, sometimes entertaining, junk sf. *Star Wars* is skiffy."

(However, the first person I heard using the pronuncia-tion, Damon Knight, used it to describe truly brainless fodder like *Battlestar Galactica*.)

Science-fiction writers have a legitimate beef against sci-fi—not only is it the bastard child of science fiction, but it gener-ates about a hundred times as much income, and one result of all that money is that lucrative movie and TV sci-fi feeds back into written science fiction, cluttering the stands with derivative crap. What's worse, those "sons-of-sci-fi" books come from the same people who publish science fiction, and come out of the same part of the publisher's resources. So we're paid less for our books, and have smaller portions of the editors' time and the publicists' budg-ets.

But I have to admit that I like good sci-fi, and have even written some of the stuff, either because of lean times or for the fun of it. I even wrote a sci-fi movie, *Robot Jox*, a less ambitious entertainment than *The Matrix* (about the way *The Simpsons* is less ambitious than *Twelfth Night*). But as exciting and complex as *The Matrix* is, I repeat, it's not science fiction.

That's not splitting hairs or being elitist. It is being dis-criminatory, in the sense of being able to discriminate between grapes and cherries. The difference between science fiction and sci-fi is as basic as the difference between poetry and greeting card verse. Both are similar in appearance but different in function; in both comparisons, the commercial manifestation trumps its intellectual brother. A sonnet on a get-well card is greeting card verse, even if it's a good sonnet. A science fiction story that takes on sci-fi characteristics becomes sci-fi, even if it's a good story.

But note this gray area: If you open a greeting card full of hearts and flowers, and inside is a sonnet by Shakespeare, you're undeniably holding a poem, as well as greeting card verse. We'll get back to that.

To me, the main characteristic of sci-fi is its indifference to science. Science fiction nowadays, post-Gernsback, may not be about science, but it's set in a rational universe where the laws of science consistently describe reality. Sci-fi normally exists in a Hollywood universe, where the laws of science have no more relevance to the product than the everyday landscape that lies hidden behind a movie director's painted backdrop.

Some sci-fi, not all of it bad, is not benignly indifferent, but actively hostile to science and engineering. Most of Spielberg's cinematic scientists, from *E.T.* to *Minority Report*, are evil caricatures or bumbling authority figures, and spiritual values always triumph over mere science and engineering. To be fair, though, a large fraction of science-fiction stories, from Mary Shelley and H. G. Wells onward, have been cautionary tales about the misuse of science.

Another consistent characteristic of sci-fi is flash, which can be thrilling if done with imagination and intelligence, and just silly if not. (Of course there are effective movies like *Galaxy Quest* and *The Rocky Horror Picture Show* that put the silliness to good comic use.)

There's good sci-fi and bad, just as there is good science fiction and bad. But their goodness and badness are determined by different criteria. Sci-fi needs action, thrills, a strong plot. Sci-fi movies want visual novelty, particularly mind-blowing special effects—which is becoming harder and harder, as movie audiences become jaded and the computation power needed for sophisticated graphics becomes cheap enough for anyone to hire.

(There's an unfortunate side effect for writers. The *Men in Black* movies made horrifically convincing aliens into such comical figures that you can't scare an audience with them anymore. It's a great loss.)

Good science fiction doesn't need action, thrills, or even strong plotting. It needs ideas and good writing. That's obviously why it's become its own progeny's stepchild. A well-written movie that makes you think might garner critical praise, but it won't make a dime on the dollar compared to a brainless sequence of explosions, breathless chase scenes, and sex, prefereably in zero-gravity.

Even sex, chases, and explosions can't financially rescue a science-fiction movie that makes you think, as *Blade Runner* painfully demonstrated. A relatively quiet, thoughtful one like *Gattaca* seems an almost quixotic enterprise, though I'm glad people keep trying.

The interesting actual sf idea in *The Matrix*, about computers becoming self-aware and taking over, is a half-century old at least: Arthur C. Clarke postulated the inevitable independence of computers in *Profiles of the Future*, written when computers were the size of warehouses and couldn't out perform a Palm Pilot.

But that idea is actual science fiction, and if *The Matrix* had been a book, written by an actual science-fiction writer, the whole story might have been rationalized into the science-fiction camp.

Let's take a look at what the "gray area" means in terms of a universe comprising all stories. Both science fiction and sci-fi are subgenres of fantasy, the word being taken in its most general sense. Some science fiction and some fantasy are quite respectable:

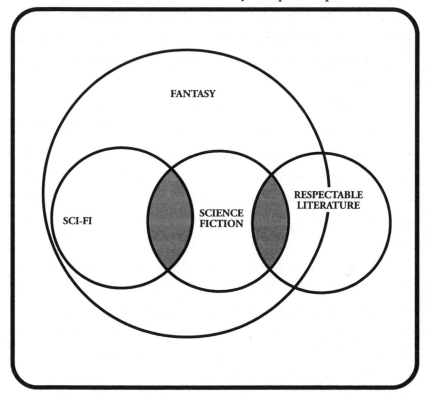

This diagram, of course, reveals my own prejudices. If *The Matrix*, tired of fame and fortune, wanted to become respectable, then the parts of it that rely on magic and faith would have to be rationalized into the science-fiction sphere. (Or, to be consistent with the diagram, by dumping the SF part completely, and becoming something like magic realism.)

The business about dodging bullets and slo-mo kung fu is no problem. As the movie says, once the humans realize that their external "reality," the Matrix, is virtual and malleable, they can bend the laws of physics to their whim. We have an elementary version of that already, in the noisiest corner of your local shopping mall. A fiction writer would explain this a little more clearly and with less mystical mumbo-jumbo than the characters in the movie, but the concept itself isn't irrational.

Elementary thermophysics would make you throw out the silliness about AI enslaving billions of humans in order to serve as energy factories, humans having clouded over the earth to deprive computers of energy. Likewise, the notion that Zion, where the remaining humans live, is near the center of the earth, where there is still some heat. (You'd be better off burning the humans' food for energy; the earth's center is going to be molten metal for a long, long time, no matter what happens on the surface.)

Any science-fiction writer could come up with something better than that. Since the folks in the movie can evidently plug themselves into computers, why not have the human race enslaved into a ten-billion-element massively parallel organic computer? Thus they supply the computing power, not the electricity, that allows the AI to survive and the Matrix to exist.

The stuff about Fate is a little harder to manage. The logic of the movie's basic storyline is that there is no free will. Neo will turn out to be The One, and he will do it by deciding to sacrifice himself for Morpheus, and Trinity will fall in love with Neo after he's dead—and the Oracle will have predicted it all ahead of time. That's a tall order, but it can still be rationalized by yet another level of virtuality: *The Matrix* is a play inside a play; a demonstration, like the play within *Hamlet*.

Thus there is a Matrix-Prime reality, after the AI villains have been put back into their metal boxes, within which *The Matrix* plays itself out as a sort of mythical metaphor explaining how humanity won its freedom back. Granted, the structure of the novel Matrix-Prime would be as murky and complicated as a Burroughs novel, and I don't mean Edgar Rice, but it would put the story back into the rational universe.

Myth and metaphor are central to the movie, anyhow. There are so many throwaway references that you can choose your favorite myth, and so much clutter lying around that you can buttress your choice no matter what it is.

Sci-fi in general is closer to myth than science fiction is. Its stories tend to be quests, involving supernatural powers and beings. That's not necessarily bad, but it can be too obvious, the ghost of Joseph Campbell guiding the hero through his phases.

The Matrix flirts with the Christian mythos without too much subtlety, Neo being Christ; Trinity, Mary Magdelene; Morpheus, John the Baptist; and Cypher, Judas. Greek mythology is pretty direct, too, since Morpheus is the controller of dreams, and Morpheus in the movie is working to free humanity from the dream world of the Matrix. Neo can also stand in for Buddha or Moses as well. Wander around the Web and you can find almost anything, including a spirited interpretation of the movie as a rebuttal of the Christian myth.

The mythology of Hollywood is evoked again and again, most

overtly in the shoot-out scene that begins the climax (with a wind-blown newspaper substituting for the tumbling tumbleweed) and Neo's apotheosis as Superman at the very end. We also have lines from *The Wizard of Oz* and *Alice in Wonderland* and the obvious homage to *Star Wars*, with Orpheus playing the part of Obi-Wan Kenobi, and to John Woo/Bruce Lee in the over-the-top fight scenes. The Agents stepped right out of *Men in Black*. True cineastes refer to "dozens" of movies that *The Matrix* borrows or steals from; these are the ones that are obvious even to me.

(To the best of my knowledge, no one has yet tried to explain the movie through the obscure mythology of science-fiction fandom, where a "neo" is someone who has been touched

by the magic of the thing but has yet to learn its language and tropes—the dirty pros and smofs, the power of fiawol and the dread of gafiation. That is a sleeping dog we shall tiptoe by.)

One throwaway reference that will probably be fueling easy masters' theses for a decade or so is the fact that Neo has his stash of illicit programs hidden in a hollowed-out book that is a basic postmodern text, *Simulacra and Simulation*, by Jean Baudrillard. Like the movie itself, postmodernism is a stimulating grab-bag of notions, not necessarily related to one another in any outside context. From the momentary flash of that book title, any half-awake graduate student can ride the white rabbit of postmodernism across the junkyard of the film's references to whatever conclusion seems most acceptable to his or her thesis committee.

That may be the best and final joke in a movie that is, in its deadpan seriousness, a funny sci-fi romp from beginning to end.

Tomorrow May Be Different

David Brin

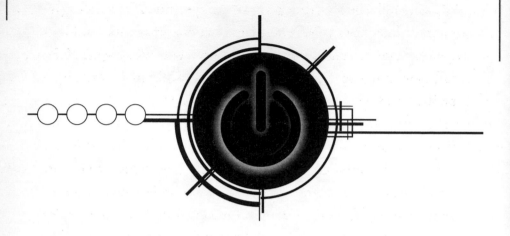

Cyberpunk: Just Another Rebellion

Back in the 1980s, the field of science fiction was all afroth over a movement that proclaimed itself as *cyberpunk*. Reviewers both inside and far outside the genre went into paroxysms over this new movement, crediting it with everything from "gritty, sharp-edged realism," to "high-gloss textures," to "inventing the trope of an angry tomorrow, symbolized by the angry young man of the streets."

Setting aside egregious exaggerations and heaps of heavy-breathing hype, this literary movement surely made the field more interesting for a while. Haughty literary mavens, who normally snub "sci-fi," condescended to discover these daring writers of dark, heroic, slashing prose, including William Gibson, author of *Neuromancer*, a tale filled with stark, vivid imagery about a future dominated by oppressive corporate structures. A future in which control over access to *information* outweighed the importance of political or military power.

It was a heady time, even for those of us who were shunted, willy-nilly, into the category of "the opposition." I was happy to grant interviews to reporters from national magazines seeking quotes from critics of the cyberpunk movement. Whatever. I dutifully played my part, double-teaming the establishment. Hey, free publicity is fine!

In retrospect, the cyberpunk movement was probably the finest free promotion campaign ever waged on behalf of science fiction. Brilliantly managed, and backed by some works of estimable value, it snared and reeled in countless new readers, while opening fresh opportunities in Hollywood and the visual arts. True, the self-important rhetoric and whines of persecution sounded ironic—at times even hilarious. However, the CP rebels did shake things up. We owe them a debt.

Ah, but were they original?

Name any point of interest in the history of Western culture, and you'll likely see a similar pattern. In retrospect, the trial of Socrates was all about a "punk" of sorts, with a reputation for extravagant behavior, satirizing standard values, and spewing unconventional new metaphors. The young writers of the Enlightenment, back in the eighteenth century, saw themselves toppling a stagnant order, using the fresh light of scientific reason to dispel superstition. Indeed, the followers of Locke and Jefferson rattled the world.

When these men grew older, and mighty in success, along came the *romantics*—typified by Shelley, Byron, and others, young men who derided Reason as an oppressive cudgel wielded by fogeys and old farts. Science was portrayed as a chain that aimed to shackle the vaulting ambitions of the human soul. Indeed, science fiction was born amid this tussle, with Mary Shelley's seminal *Frankenstein*, emerging literally in the middle of the Romantic movement, containing within it SF's perpetual answer to romanticism—that progress will happen and the only way to deal with it will be wisdom.

The Romantic movement was more, of course, than simply cultural recidivism—more than a grandson allying himself with his grandfather in common hatred of papa. Predictability would take all the fun out of being a rebel! Still, there is a certain inevitability about these cycles. There will never be a shortage of young men and women, eager to announce new revelations. No matter how fine the accomplishments of their parents, bright newcomers will always be ready to proclaim themselves prophets of a new age.

All the more so for the loose confederacy of genres known as *speculative fiction*! After all, SF is the literature *of* change—in the human condition and in the universe as a whole. By its nature, it must encourage fresh ideas or perish.

So SF had the "New Wave" authors of the sixties—Ellison, Zelazny, Silverberg—who decried the prior emphasis on gadgetry and plot, proclaiming the discovery of something called *style*. Language became their palette. Their colors would be passion, stirred in the reader's soul.

Naturally, the Old Farts thought a lot of this was straight bull. They had spent half a lifetime ardently fighting for the freedom to speculate about mankind's relationship with technology and space and time—and now these young whippersnappers were just taking that freedom for granted. Worse, they were strutting about as if *they* were the true innovators!

Indeed, the best New Wave writers were wonderfully inventive, contributing something vital to our genre, just when it was needed most. They raised new issues, posed new quandaries, precisely because those prior battles had been won. The *best* of the old guard did not grouse when the newcomers came by, flaunting new, gaudy plumage. Rather, they smiled, remembering what it was to be young. And they said, "Come on over here, son. Sit down and tell me all about it."

So it was with cyberpunk in the Eighties. Although I was younger than most of the CP folk, and started my career much more recently, somehow I found myself in the OF (Old Farts) camp, perhaps because I truly do believe that technology and reason will play a role in raising generations better than ours. Assigned a role, I was only too glad to play along for the fun of it, keeping quiet to outsider reporters about the fact that I *really* liked most of the work I'd read by William Gibson, Bruce Sterling, and Pat Cadigan—and had already contributed my own gritty, noir bits to the trend.

Ah, well. As literary movements go, cyberpunk is already well past ripe middle age. Like some of its practitioners, who can be seen occasionally peering into each others' mirror-shades suspiciously, watching age-lines and liver spots emerge. But the worst is coming. For the most successful movements are always punished by becoming . . . clichés.

Consider the story of the elderly lady who was taken to her first Shakespeare play ever—*Hamlet*. Her reaction? "Well, I thought it was very nice . . . but it was all so full of quotations!" Such is the doom of authors, to be fated at one end with obscurity, and at the other end, after success, with being copied until everyone is sick of you. Alas.

And each successful generation creates something else . . . a *new* clade of rebels, fomenting revolution and rejection against the prior one. Bright kids who are talking about these new things they've discovered . . . things called "story," and "character," and "hope."

Many people have tried to define science fiction. I like to call it the literature of exploration and *change*. While other genres obsess upon so-called eternal verities, SF deals with the possibility that our children may have different problems. They may, indeed, *be* different than we have been.

Change is an important matter—it's the salient feature of our age. How well do *you* deal with change?

All creatures live embedded in time, though only human beings seem to lift their heads to comment on this fact, lamenting the past or worrying over what's to come. Our brains are uniquely equipped to handle this temporal *skepsis*. For example, twin neural clusters that reside just above our eyes—the prefrontal lobes—appear especially adapted for extrapolating ahead.

Meanwhile, swathes of older cortex can flood with vivid memories of yesterday, triggered by the merest sensory tickle, as when a single aromatic whiff sent Proust back to roam his mother's kitchen for eighty thousand words. (We'll return to neurons and the brain, later.)

Obsession with either past or future can almost define a civilization. Worldwide, most cultures believed in some lost golden age when people knew more, when they mused *loftier thoughts* and were closer to the gods—but then fell from that state of grace. The myth occurred so frequently, in so many continents and so many contexts—despite an almost complete lack of credible evidence for any genuine past "golden age"—that we must assume the fable wells up from something basic in our natures.

Under this dour but recurrent "look-back" worldview, men and women of a later, coarser era can only look back with envy to that better, happier time, studying ancient lore and hoping to live up to remnants of ancient wisdom.

Just a few societies dared contradict this standard dogma of nostalgia. Our own Scientific West, with its impudent notion of progress, brashly relocated any "golden age" to the future, something to work *toward*, a human construct for our grandchildren to achieve with craft, sweat and good will—assuming that we manage to prepare them properly for such an ambitious task. Implicit is the postulate that our offspring can and should be better than us, a glimmering hope that is nurtured (a bit) by two generations of steadily rising IQ scores.

This perspective can be important when we examine popular mythologies in the realm of science fiction. Take a number of popular epics: for example, *The Matrix*, *Minority Report*, and *Blade Runner*, the latter two films inspired by literary works of Philip K. Dick.

We shall see that these works—and others, such as *Star Wars*, *The Lord of the Rings*, and the perennial, *Star Trek*—can be especially well illuminated by asking the following questions:

1. Does the work look forward to human progress or does it push nostalgia by lamenting a lost golden age?

2. Is *science* portrayed with loathing? Or is it seen as a hopeful trend that must also be watched care-

fully against harmful excess?

3. What role does *rebellion* play? Is suspicion of authority portrayed as a private thing? (The hero as a lone fox among sheep.) Or is suspicion of authority portrayed as a healthy reaction by all citizens, who participate by helping to keep the mighty accountable?

4. Are "heroes" portrayed as normal people—perhaps above-average, but part of the human continuum? Or are they demigods, exalted above common humanity by class or genes or even by divine right?

These are not the usual literary categories applied by analytical critics, but I am willing to wager that they will prove enlightening. First, however, let us begin with one obvious fact, that every generation is invaded by a new wave of barbarians—its children.

Why Rebel?

Do you believe that the people around you are subjected to propaganda? Most people think so. Please take a moment to write down on a piece of paper which campaign you think most thoroughly indoctrinates your fellow citizens. Some mention Communism, religion, or consumer advertising . . . or that today's mass media push *conformity* on a hapless, sheeplike population.

It is a smug cliché—that you alone (or perhaps with a few friends)—happen to see through the conditioning that has turned all the rest into passively obedient sheep. Cyberpunk plays to this image by portraying a lone individual—or perhaps just a few—scurrying like rats under the dark towers of the ruling masters. In

The Matrix, the masters are evil computers. In *Johnny Mnemonic*, they are the rulers of faceless corporations. In *The X-Files*, it is a government conspiracy. What these myths share in common is the grimly satisfying image that the masses are useless bystanders, lowing and mooing in confusion.

In fact, it never occurs to the heroes of these tales (above all *The X-Files*) to actually appeal to the very masses who pay the hero's wages and deserve his loyal respect. The common man or woman cannot help resist the Dark Power, because they were long ago indoctrinated into dull, unquestioning obedience.

Ah, but here is the ironic twist. Look around yourself. I'll bet you cannot name, offhand, a single popular film of the last forty years that actually preached homogeneity, submission, or

repression of the individual spirit.

That's a clue!

In fact, the most persistent and inarguably incessant prop-aganda campaign, appearing in countless movies, novels, myths and TV shows, preaches quite the opposite! A singular and unswerving theme so persistent and ubiquitous that most people hardly notice or mention it. And yet, when I say it aloud, you will nod your heads in instant recognition.

That theme is *suspicion of authority*—often accompanied by its sidekick/partner: *tolerance.*

Indeed, try to come up with even one example of a recent film you enjoyed in which the hero did not bond with the audi-ence in the first ten minutes by resisting or sticking it to some authority figure.

Some filmmakers, such as Steven Spielberg, use this potent cinematic ingredient in measured doses, creating and por-traying authority figures who are just malevolent and powerful enough to keep the heroes in jeopardy, without too much exag-geration. Others slather on the authoritarian premise as thick as sugar icing in a wedding cake, using the sweetness of resentment to overwhelm all other lacks in plot or consistency or taste.

Alas, the latter tendency is all too frequent in SF cinema. Take the bleak paranoia that pervades *The Matrix* and other films of its genre. Oh, I don't mind some tales about rebellion against mega-computers. What gets tedious is the relentless refusal ever to recognize—and then start cleverly varying—a classic cliché.

But back to the essence here. Rebels are always the heroes. Conformity is portrayed as worse than death. Even in war flicks, irreverence for some pompous commander is a necessary trait.

Often, the main character also presents some quirky trait, some eccentricity, that draws both ire from some oppressor and sympathy from the audience.

Oh, you do hear *some* messages of conformity and intolerance—but these fill the mouths of moustache-twirling villains, clearly inviting us to rebel contrary to everything they say. Submission to gray tribal normality is portrayed as one of the most contemptible things an individual can do—a message quite opposite to what was pushed in most other cultures.

This theme is so prevalent, and so obvious, that even though you can see where I am going with it—and hate the inevitable conclusion—you aren't going to dispute the core fact. You have to sit there and accept one of the most galling things that a bunch of dedicated individualists can ever realize: That you were *trained* to be individualists by the most relentless campaign of public indoctrination in history, suckling your love of rebellion and eccentricity from a society that—evidently, at some level—*wants* you to be that way!

Oh, the ironies abound.

A Question of Perspective

So, do all popular works of fiction promote suspicion of authority? At some level, yes they do. It is the core element of the modern drama, showing just how far the modern sensibility has traveled, parting markedly from the passive plaints of poor doomed Oedipus and Othello, who had no recourse when they were marked for agony by their gods. The classical Greeks, Romans, Japanese, and others tended to portray resistance as futile—as prescribed primly in Aristotle's *Poetics*—a fundamental tenet of the

"Look Back" view mentioned earlier.

In contrast, some modern SF and fantasy tales aggressively take the extreme opposite position. Take *Xena* and *Hercules*, two fairly lowbrow popular television series in which authority figures were portrayed as evil in direct proportion to their rudeness or callousness toward common folk. Xena might rescue an exiled king from invaders and restore his throne, but only if he treats people nicely and promises to set up a democratically elected city council. Any time someone is abused by an Olympian, that "god" is sure to face dire punishment from our heroine!

Ah, but the will toward worshipping Olympians and demigods still roils within us. After all, we spent thousands of years in feudal settings that were totally undemocratic. Social structures were pyramid-shaped, with a narrow elite dominating ignorant masses. Starting with Homer's *Iliad* and *Gilgamesh,* nearly all of the bards and storytellers worked for the chiefs, aristocrats and kings who owned all the marbles. (A point conveniently never mentioned by Joseph Campbell in *The Hero's Journey*.) Naturally they preached that lords and "better" folk had a right to exercise capricious power at whim. You could choose which demigod to root for—say, Achilles or Hector. But there was no disputing the super-hero's ultimate right to deal with mortals however he wished.

Of course this is another aspect of the nostalgic-romantic Look Back worldview. Today you see it exemplified in two highly popular epics, the Ender series of Orson Scott Card and the *Star Wars* saga produced by George Lucas. In both, the pivotal characters are born profoundly superior to those around them . . . not just a little smarter, but indisputably and qualitatively greater than the mere mortals surrounding them. Moreover, the distinction is not one earned by hard work or the give-and-take of reciprocal criticism that typifies modern teamwork, democracy, meritocracy or science. Rather the justification is one of inherited genetic supremacy, giving the hero an inherent right to meddle at will.

Nearly all O. S. Card works feature a central demigod, whose saving grace is a deep self-pitying angst—expressed at great length—over being forced to over-rule the obstinate will of benighted humanity and set things straight. But at least Card's characters seem to feel vague regret that people aren't able to handle things as adults. Not bothering with such hand-wringing, George Lucas's "Jedi Force" mythology baldly and openly extols the same sort of secretive mystical priest-class that assisted and excused oppressive kings in nearly all eras, on nearly all continents. And all the while, both sagas put forward strawman "authority figures" for the characters to resent openly, while real manipulators play the underlying dance tune.

Of course, the very notion of progress is anathema to nostalgic-romantics. Despite techie furnishings, the *Star Wars* pop-epic relentlessly preaches the nostalgist party line—an ideal society ought to be ruled by secretive-mystical elites, unaccountable and self-chosen based on inherent qualities of blood. The only good knowledge is old knowledge. (No wonder it all happened "long ago, in a galaxy far away.")

Note: These romantics needn't be anti-technological, though they almost have to reject science. Their worldview is utterly incompatible with the way science works or thinks.

From Virgil and the Vedas to Plato, Shelley and Tolkien, all the way to Updike and Rowling, this prevalent nostalgist tradition spanned five continents and forty centuries. Some rage, others fizz; but all grumble at tomorrow.

Even where the heroes of these tales practice "suspicion of authority" (they must, in order to bond with today's audiences) the dispute is portrayed as one among demigods. Mere mortals have the option of dying as spear carriers—as they did in the *Iliad*—and of worshipping the demigods with mass ceremonies, as in *Triumph of the Will*.

Contrast this with the view portrayed in *Star Trek*, in which democracy is an inherent good. Scientific progress, while deserving skeptical oversight, is seen as both inevitable and probably desirable. The ship's captain, while great, relies utterly on the competence of his or her "merely human" crew, any one of whom may prove crucial and deserving of a brief moment on center stage.. In *Star Trek*, any demigod is viewed with worried doubt. (For more on this distinction, see http://www.davidbrin.com/star-warsarticle1.html)

Frankly, I am amazed that *Star Trek* ever thrived. Certainly it is unsurprising to find that its core element of progressive optimism has seldom been emulated elsewhere in the canon of SF. There are a few other examples. Robert Silverberg, Iain Banks, and Wil McCarthy have been known to portray futures in which our descendants face problems commensurately difficult enough to challenge even people who are far better and wiser than we are.

Let's face it; portraying a smart future civilization—one that nevertheless faces cleverly onerous problems—can be hard work! It is much, much easier to milk the emotions by using a demigod character, in a dystopian setting filled with clueless citizens. Just assume the worst about society and give the readers or viewers the emotional satisfaction of watching that supreme hero "rebel" against some garishly simple and overwrought authority figure . . . while at the same time wielding magical forces that he was born with and destined to use.

The Difficulty of Optimism

Where do many of today's popular genre films fit in?

Take *The Matrix,* a movie I quite enjoyed! Its high-tech premise and cyber-glossy ambiance are lavishly attractive and the conflict setup is appealing. Who could resist the dark glamour of its design, the pyrotechnics of its stunts, the seduction of its noir-ish vision?

Above all, relish the classic audience identification with a character who is told in advance that he will be "The One" . . . and any skill that he lacks—any skill that *you* ever wished that you had time to learn—can be downloaded in a matter of seconds! (Naturally, this miracle uses the very same science that the central premise preaches to have been one big mistake. Ironies are another lavish trait of the film.)

But how does it score according to the four questions I posed earlier?

On almost every count, *The Matrix,* is an unabashedly nostalgic-romantic piece, loyal to the elitist, look backward world-view, suspicious of science and deeply contemptuous of the masses, which are portrayed more sheeplike here than in any other work of popular culture! Only at the very end is there a hint that perhaps the common man or woman might someday be wakened from their seductive slumbers. But not much chance of that.

(Don't get me wrong! Dark warnings are among the greatest literary works and SF does civilization a genuine good when it dourly explores potential failure modes. Elsewhere I go into the importance of self-preventing prophecies—SF tales that have quite possibly saved our lives and certainly helped save freedom, by innoculating a definitely NOT-sheeplike public with heightened awareness of a potential danger. Among the greatest of these were *Dr. Strangelove, Soylent Green,* and *Nineteen Eighty-Four,* all of which helped make the author's vivid warning somewhat obsolete through the unexpected miracle that people actually listened.)

Still, there have been enough paeans of praise for the style and the warning inherent in *The Matrix.* I want to go back to those under-discussed aspects—such as the devout adherence to a nostalgist-romantic-Look Back way of viewing the world.

Contrast this mentality with another enjoyable romp—*The Fifth Element*—a far less serious or thoughtful film than *The Matrix*—one whose general mindlessness is only matched by its unabashed joy. Ebullience and optimism spills off the screen in gushing torrents, overwhelming the viewer's sense of surly skepticism, even when the adventure is at its most dire or the plot is most ridiculous. True, there is a demigod . . . but she desperately needs the aid and succor of mere mortal heroes, even citizens who are passing by! Some authority figures drive the plot with their vileness, but the director does not feel it necessary to tar all of society and all of science with this brush. The villains are plenty bad enough. No need to make the cake all frosting.

Take another example—*Minority Report . . .* or almost any Steven Spielberg film, for that matter. Spielberg is unabashedly progressive and loyal to the Look Forward *zeitgeist.* Although he skillfully utilizes suspicion-of-authority, he cannot let himself fall for the *X Files* cliché of a country and citizenry that are completely and forever clueless. Even the government—a classic target of authority-resentment in film—is never portrayed as unalloyedly vile. Rather, his abusive authority figures are narrowly defined, a vile police chief here . . . a callous scientist there.

Moreover, the hero can even sometimes call upon help from decent people and institutions. While there are moments of techno-Orwellian creepiness in *Minority Report*, such as when the police send spy-eye "spiders" running through an apartment building, Spielberg portrays this as a highly limited invasion, one that sovereign citizens have clearly decided to put up with. They can still vote to eliminate a particular police power if they decide they do not like it—in fact this is a central element to the plot. This future may be creepy and filled with problems, but it is no clichéd tyranny.

In other words, unlike George Lucas, Spielberg is grateful to a civilization of democracy, egalitarian science and general decency. He simply cannot bring himself to spit in its face. Especially not after it has been so good to him.

The Roots of Fantasy

At the very opposite extreme, consider the popularity of feudal/magical fantasies, of the kind typified by *The Lord of the Rings*

Recall how a core element of romanticism is to spurn the modern emphasis on pragmatic experimentation, production, universal literacy, cooperative enterprise and flattened social orders. In contrast to these "sterile" pursuits, Romantics extolled the traditional, the personal, the particular, the subjective and metaphorical. Consider how this fits with the very plot of *The Lord of the Rings*, in which the good guys strive to win re-establishment of an older, graceful and "natural" hierarchy against the disturbing, quasi-industrial and vaguely technological ambience of Mordor, with its smokestack imagery and manufactured power-rings that can be used by anybody, not just an elite few. Those man-made wonders are deemed cursed, damning anyone who dares to use them, usurping the rightful powers of their betters (the high elves).

Another of the really cool things about fantasy—you can identify with a side that's one hundred percent pure, distilled good and revel as they utterly annihilate foes who *deserve* to be exterminated because they are one hundred percent evil! This may not be politically correct, but then political correctness is really a bastard offspring of egalitarian-scientific enlightenment. Romanticism never made any pretense at equality. It is hyper-discriminatory, by nature.

The urge to crush some demonized enemy resonates deeply within us, dating from ages far earlier than feudalism. Hence, the vicarious thrill we feel over the slaughter of orc foot soldiers at Helm's Deep. Then again as the Ents flatten even more goblin grunts at Saruman's citadel, taking no prisoners, without a thought for all the orphaned orclings and grieving widorcs. And again at Minas Tirith, and again at the Gondor docks and again . . . well, they're only orcs, after all. What fun.

Notice any similarity to the waves of foot-soldiers and spear carriers who died under Achilles's hand in the *Iliad* . . . or in the *Star Wars* saga?

Among all the attempts to cast definitions of fantasy and science fiction, to help explain the chasm that so many see, let me offer this one based on the difference between the Look Back and

Look Forward worldviews.

Science fiction is the genre that posits the slim possibility that children might—sometimes—be capable of learning from the mistakes of their parents. That people may someday be better than us, even partly on account of our efforts. They may no longer need kings. They may, each of them, be capable of rising up and being heroes.

A Continuing Struggle of Worldviews

There is no resolution to this ongoing struggle, one that runs deeper than any politics or ideology. Movies such as *The Matrix* and *Minority Report* embody this struggle. While we are entranced by the similarities, the glossy, diverting futures and techno-wonders and dark warnings, it is important also to remember that there are deeper assumptions at play. Assumptions about what human beings can potentially achieve.

Science fiction, in effect, has become a central battlefield in one of the most important disputes roiling in the human mind—the decision whether to continue our obsession with hierarchies, demigods and the past . . . or to turn with confidence and wary optimism toward the future.

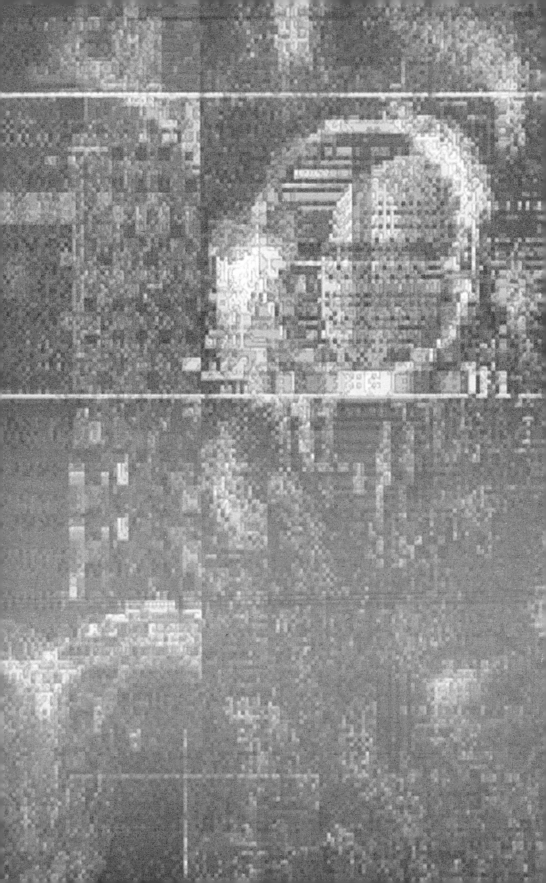

Revenge of the Nerds, Part X

Alan Dean Foster

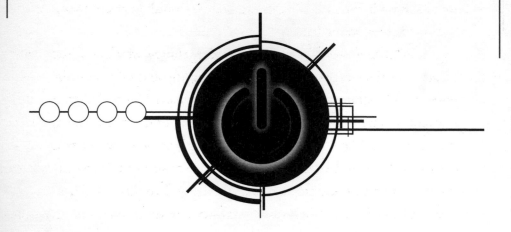

D o you remember that one special, overriding feeling you had when you were a kid? No, not the cool taste of good ice cream, or the laughter of friends, or the warmth inherent in your mother's kitchen. Not those. Nothing so amenable. I'm talking about fear. The constant, overriding feeling of helplessness. Of never being in control, no matter how hard you tried, of any part of your environment. Of always being dominated by everything and everyone around you. The feeling of being afraid—of your parents, your older siblings, the bully at school (there is always a bully at school), of strangers at a family gathering, of strangers on a city street. Of strangers everywhere. Of the whole world. Not to mention The Horror In the Closet, The Monster Under the Bed, The Lurker Outside Your Bedroom Window—and Uncle Jake's bulging eyes, affectionately pinching fingers, and decomposing breath. Calm down. Be at ease. You are not alone. We were all afraid of those things (some of us still are—

particularly of Uncle Jake), and there was nothing, absolutely positively know-it-for-sure-all nothing, that we could do about them.

But we wanted to.

Oh, how we wanted to! How desperately we desired the means and the wherewithal to contemptuously and effortless dispose of bully, strangers, Thing in Closet, Monster Under Bed, and Lurker Outside Window—and, to our secret but delicious shame, probably Uncle Jake as well (but not Aunt Jane, who baked nice cookies). We could not. Why not? Because we were invariably smaller, weaker, less experienced, dumber, and too afraid. These powerful, atavistic emotions from childhood never leave us entirely, no matter how mature or "grown-up" we think we have become. Perhaps not in reality (at least not too often, fortunately) but certainly in fantasy, who hasn't at one time or another wanted to kill the boss, or the jerk down the street who always goes out of his way to make sure his dog dumps on *your* lawn, or the prattling idiot of a politician staring out of the TV who we know is flat out lying to our faces, or the amoral CEO who's responsible for shoveling poor old folks' life savings into the nearest trash can while on his way to St. Tropez for yet another "business conference"?

But it's among children, and particularly among those adrift in the Sargasso Sea of their teen years, where these emotions run deepest. Where every day is devoted to minimize the mental and emotional paper cuts of fear and helplessness. Which is why that particular segment of the film-going public responded so readily and enthusiastically to *The Matrix*.

Because despite what you see on the big screen *The Matrix*, while nominally science fiction and more specifically drawing upon the sub-genre of that literature known as cyberpunk, is not about computers or evil machines enslaving humankind or even really cool shades. It's about the empowerment of the not quite adult. People can write all they want about the film's mirror-shade slant and slick special effects, about its mysterious message and loosely plotted framing tale of the machines of the future enslaving the species, but what it really does is send out a message to every teenager in the audience (and most especially to the male portion) that at least in the world of *The Matrix*, you too—you nerdy, sallow, pimple-faced, skinny, unathletic lump of malleable human stuff—you too can exert Godlike control over each and every one of your tormentors. And get the girl, to boot (up).

Spend time in a theater showing the film, observe this much sought after audience segment, and you can see it in their eyes. In ways no teen male can identify with Schwarzenegger or Stallone (or Vin Diesel), they can see themselves as Keanu Reeves/Neo. It's a lead role the producers were oh-so-clever in casting. Reeves is trim without being buff, athletic without being imposing or overawing, handsome without being too pretty. Unlike Arnold or Sly or Vin, it is entirely possible to envision him having actually suffered from acne. The boys in the audience can identify with him, can see themselves *as* him. Physically, Neo is far more skateboarder than shooting guard. With his leaps and kicks and somersaults, he's Extreme Sports before the term was coined. He's not big, he's not muscular, he's no hulk. He even looks like a slightly aged teenager. There are no lines in his face. The stress he shows on screen is mental, inner, confused. The kind of predicament those in the audience can sense because they've experienced it themselves. So different from Eastwood worrying about capturing the kidnapper, or

Schwarzenegger agonizing over how to blow up the drug cartel's headquarters.

Few teens see themselves ever engaging in such outrageous, outsized, Hollywoodized actions. But being hauled away from one's computer to face a room full of hostile adults, *that* they can empathize with. Hugo Weaving, in a marvelous performance as the lead "Agent" of the evil machine program, is no lumbering Richard Kiel as Jaws, no squat and invincible Oddjob. Physically and mentally, he's about as far from the typical cinematic "big" as Kasparov is from Kurt Warner. Instead, his character is every nasty high-school vice principal, school bully, and supercilious, overbearing adult a typical teenager encounters all rolled into one. The interrogation room into which he and his supporting agents toss the bewildered Neo is every principal's office and every "let's beat the crap out of him!" behind-the-school back alley any put-upon kid ever had the misfortune to visit. It's critical to the success of *The Matrix*'s appeal that the audience fully identifies with Neo at such moments, even when he's *not* wiping up the cyberfloor with the bad guys. What teenage boy identifies with the "plight" of Arnold trapped in the jungle lair of an evil arms merchant, or James Bond stuck in a holding cell in the wilds of Southeast Asia? But put him in a dull, featureless room with a bunch of hostile, stony-visaged adults looming over him and quizzing him relentlessly about things he doesn't understand—well, it's welcome to my nightmare time, sings (not Carroll's) Alice.

In many teenage boys' revenge fantasies, he's not alone. There is always a sidekick; someone bigger than the bully, smarter than the adults, more simpatico than the school administrators. In *The Matrix* this role is fulfilled by Laurence Fishburne's

Morpheus. Morpheus is Chewbacca with an advanced degree: big, strong, tough, but also knowledgeable. He's mentor and protector all rolled into one, a favorite social studies teacher—only with muscles. Not only can he kick sand right back into the faces of the bullies at the beach, he can also outthink and outtalk their interfering parents.

So what if we don't know what he's talking about half the time? Isn't that how it is with every kid's favorite teacher? It doesn't matter if the put-upon student doesn't understand him. What's important isn't Morpheus's knowledge: It's his empathy. He *cares* about Neo. He wants him to succeed. Like any good professor, he hopes his student will surpass him and feels only joy at the prospect. What more could a confused teen stumbling and bumbling his way through life and school want of a teacher? It's the rare father who tells his son that he hopes his offspring will grow up to be smarter than he is. Richer, yeah—but smarter? Teens may identify with Neo, but they reserve their affection for Morpheus.

And then there's Trinity. Wears leather. Kicks bad guy butt and early on takes out the baddies picking on poor Neo. *Knows computers.* This last is critical to her appeal to the film's target audience. It says to them that not only can a geek get a babe, you can find one who speaks your language. And she doesn't ask for anything. Doesn't demand that Neo drive a fancy car, doesn't insist he buy her dinner at some fancy restaurant where the waiter will invariably look down his nose at you because you invariably mismatch your clothes, doesn't insult him because he didn't pay for extra butter on the popcorn at the movie. She's just—there. When Neo needs her. Despite her knowledge and abilities she doesn't babble on about stuff, much less *girl* stuff.

The last thing a teenage boy wants in a girlfriend is complexity (the first thing he wants is boobs, but not even Trinity is perfect). Trinity's about as uncomplex as can be. Watching her on screen, you half get the feeling that if you met her in person and said "Hello" she'd respond with "Press Enter to activate conversation program." Even better, she doesn't have any stupid girlfriends around to giggle and point fingers and make fun of you (presumably they're all stashed away in the sleeping pods built by the evil machines). As for her attitude toward physical affection, well, when she and Neo blast their way into the skyscraper where Morpheus is being held, in an attempt to rescue him from the Agents' interrogation, he and she are having sex—with guns. Check out the look they exchange in the elevator. Positively cyber-orgasmic. One thinks "orgy at an NRA convention" (perhaps one should not). We'll leave the endless-reservoir-of-expended-shells-as-ejaculated-sperm analogy for another time.

So, what do we have here? One kindly, worldly-wise, butt-kicking mentor and one selfless, coolly affectionate, butt-kicking girlfriend—both of whom understand, use, and practically salivate over computers and their capabilities. Can you see *The Matrix*'s audience leaning forward in their seats with baited breath and intense interest as Arnold or Sly or Vin labor over a keyboard? You have to develop the appropriate characters to *fit* the cyber-setting, and the *The Matrix* does so superbly.

Finally, we come back to Neo himself. Keanu Reeves not as Steve Reeves but as Everynerd. As every smart and almost-smart kid who was ever pushed around behind the football stands during Phys Ed. That's how he starts out: baffled, bemused, and pushed around by bullies and authority. Until aforementioned mentor and girlfriend arrive to enlighten and assist him. Not only that, but to inform him that he's The One. Name me one sixteen-year-old boy who doesn't think, at some time or another, that he's The One.

Sure, you don't got no muscles. Sure, you'll never make the football team or get to lay the cheerleader. But hey, you're president of the computer club. Or the chess team. Or first in line for that academic scholarship. All of which is great, but doesn't let you take revenge on your tormentors. *The Matrix* does. The meek may not inherit the Earth, but cyberspace, that's another matter (so to speak).

What kid wouldn't want to be Neo, gifted with true understanding of how the world is really run and supplied with the means to manipulate it? You too can out-martial arts the bad guys—with the proper training. You too can blow them away with every type of weapon imaginable—with proper training. And finally, eventually, you too can defeat them by sheer force of will and make them look silly while doing it—with proper training. And how do you acquire this vital training? Through hard work at school, long hours spent sweating over the computer or pouring through thick volumes in the library, asking detailed questions of those more knowledgeable than yourself (i.e., adults)? Huh-uh. Not in *The Matrix*. There's an easier way. One that won't tax your mind, take up your valuable free time (used for playing video games or going to the movies or just hanging out), or require you to actually confront an adult with a serious question.

You just download the information directly to your brain.

The direct downloading of information to the mind has long since become an old trope in science fiction. But not in film.

While the concept may seem new and fresh to their (non-SF reading) parents, it's something teens growing up with MP3 and in-home CD burning can readily identify with, often to the consternation of their elders. Which makes this particular bit of tempting technological dream fluff proffered by *The Matrix* all that more appealing. Talk about teenage wish fulfillment! Every teenage boy would like to be able to take two things away from the pretend world of *The Matrix*. The first is an ability to simply, easily, and effortlessly download knowledge. No more studying, no more books, no more teacher's sanitation-challenged looks. Just plug in the right storage chip and hit the mental equivalent of "Save As." Learn to fly a helicopter. How to defy gravity. Absurdly balletic gunplay in one easy lesson. And all with your eyes closed, relaxing

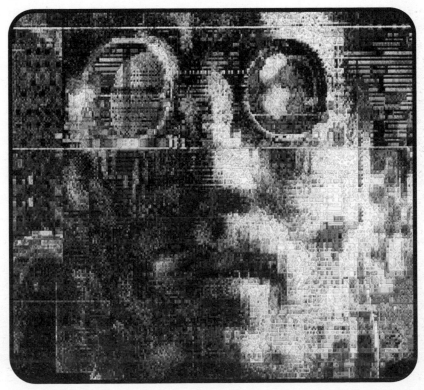

in a nice, comfy chair. All that's missing from this crucial scene in *The Matrix* is an open cooler at Neo's right hand overflowing with chilled brewskis.

And the second thing? Surprise—it's not Trinity. Not the girl, no. Number Two on our eager young geek's Matrix dream want list is that endless white background Neo calls up that's filled with row upon row, shelf upon shelf, of heavy ordinance—a testosterone-slathered wish-dream come true if ever one appeared on film. That's also where and when Reeves utters the movie's seminal line on behalf of all oppressed and misunderstood nerds. "I'll need guns—lots of guns." Of course, by the end of the story guns have been rendered superfluous by Neo's mastery of cyber-space—excuse me, of the Matrix. By comprehending its workings and fully understanding his place within them, he can now stop programs-as-bullets in mid-flight and pluck them out of the air, or cause them to fall harmlessly at his feet. The implication is that Neo's mastery of the Matrix now exceeds that of its malevolent mechanical devisers, a realization that frightens (if a program element can be frightened) the Matrix's Agents. How will they fight back against Neo's apotheosis in *The Matrix Reloaded* and *The Matrix Revolutions*? I predict the insertion into the sequels of a special kind of anti-Neo computer virus.

By the end of the film, our surrogate teenager Neo has attained complete mastery of the world around him. The fact that it isn't the real world doesn't faze him, nor does it mute the sense of identification the movie inculcates in its exhausted but exultant teen viewers. Having grown up immersed in television, movies, video games, and the Internet, they understand the difference between mastering a fantasy world and competing in the real one.

The problem is that the former is far simpler than the latter. Sometimes confusion results, to the detriment of the individual so seduced, and then we are subjected to a few days of screaming, sensation-seeking, foaming-at-the-mouth tabloid headlines. I'm still waiting for the first one:

"High School Honors Student Thinks Real World Is Nothing More Than A Computer Program! Attempts To Delete Parents!"

The Matrix not only makes its young viewers feel good by choosing as its star someone far easier for them to identify with than the archetypal Hollywood hero; it makes them feel good about *themselves* and about who they are. The message is that if Neo can do it, so can you. His perceived world is a sham, a mistake, a carefully crafted fake, and you know, deep down, that yours is, too. He exists in isolation (no parents, no wife, no girlfriend) and most teenage boys do, too. Though put-upon by others who intend him only ill, he triumphs through sheer force of brainpower and will. Arise, ye geeks of the world, for only you know the truth! Therein lies the message of *The Matrix*, and the real source of its success.

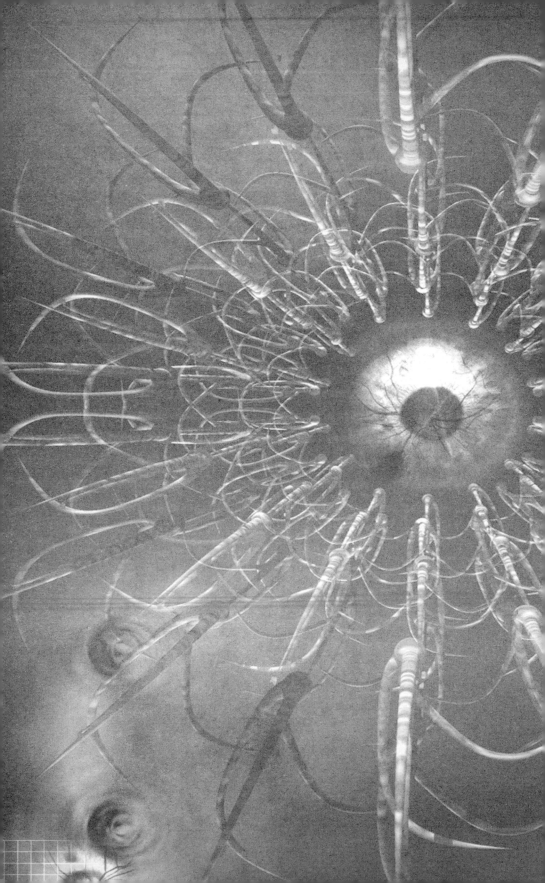

Reflections in a Cyber Eye

Karen Haber

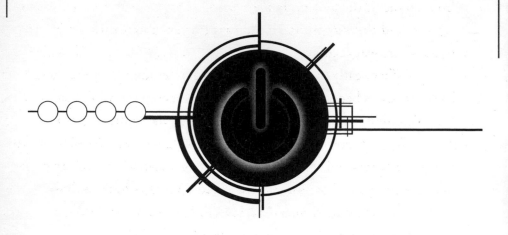

I t all begins—and ends—with black leather, doesn't it? And somehow we always knew that it would, too.

From the very first stunning moment of the very first astounding stunt scene in *The Matrix*, the viewer knows that she/he is in for a giddy funhouse ride of a movie, and, even more pointedly, a no-holds-barred stylefest.

If the late Diana Vreeland, the terrifyingly chic doyenne of *Vogue* magazine to whom even that fashion icon, Jackie Kennedy Onassis, deferred, had seen *The Matrix* she surely would have bowed to the Brothers Wachowski. Like knows like, and with *The Matrix*, the Brothers W took the style crown away from fellow moviemakers Luc Besson and Ridley Scott.

Whatever the components of style are—confidence, cool, grace and don't forget black leather—*The Matrix* has it in abundance. Long after the confusing tangle of storyline and goofy/mystical multi-culti mixed media references of the movie have faded from memory, the look remains.

And that's appropriate. All that matters about this movie, really, is the way it looks.

When, early on in the film, the character known as Trinity levitates, knees bent, and proceeds to kick the crap out of the bad guys—fulfilling at least *this* former adolescent tomboy's every dream of grace, power, and catsuits—the style bar was raised for design concept and special effects in science-fiction cinema. Filmmakers everywhere, after they located their jaws in the rubble on the floor and closed them, surely must have thought: "How in hell am I ever going to match this, much less top it?"

The Matrix confirms what some of us have always known—and feared—deep in the most secret blood-red chamber of our throbbing hearts.

Style is all that matters.

Always has been.

Always will be.

The Matrix is a glorious, triumphant celebration of style, wallowing in all of those guilty pleasures: speed, smarts, separate-but-equal trench coats, dark glasses, super powers, paranoia and, oh, yes, don't forget the guns. If anyone has ever been guilty of making guns sexy, it's the Wachowskis. The NRA should have sent the brothers free lifetime memberships with a letter of gratitude.

In this movie, guns become a *di rigeur* fashion accessory. (Matrix fashion tip #1: Girls, going on a rescue mission? Don't be caught without at least a Luger under your trench coat.)

The Matrix is a many splendored visual feast because it was magnificently conceived at ground level. Has *any* other SF movie ever had such meticulously wrought, print-ready, beautiful storyboards done by such talents as Geof Darrow and Steve Skroce? And has any other movie brought said storyboards to life with such faithful virtuousity? *The Matrix* breaks right through the frame of the comic book panel, taking its action outside the box, outside the stereotyped imagery of other SF films, into a new realm. Now *that's* dancin', as a Mr. Astaire once said.

The visual audacity of this film—as the tropes of animé are literally brought to cyberlife—overwhelms the content, message, and, thankfully, the dialog. The power of the image rules here, and the imagination behind it makes it possible to appreciate this flick even as a silent movie.

The wonderful sexy use of rearview mirrors, doorknobs, spoons, all manner of reflections, and multiple images in video screens, could have come out of a fashion video or commercial. Slick. Clever. Oh-so-knowing. So many oddly slanted perspectives working to increase the viewer's sense of dislocation, and hint at Neo's literal dislocation. What was that shadow in the mirror? That strange flicker out of the corner of your eye's reflection?

Even when Neo is literally *bugged* during the horrifying interrogation scene, the horror is made that much more harrowing by its slick stylization.

Even the bad guys are stylish: Agent Smith and his cookie-cutter fellow agents truly bring the notion of "evil suits" to cyber life with their bad haircuts, matching jackets, and slip-sliding monotonic morphability.

The machines themselves, those AI baddies, are the culmination of every bad boy dream. What at first seemed to be a stylistic non-sequitur is, in fact, a gleeful indulgence in making every viewer cringe. Nasty. If these machines don't look like spiders then they look like mosquitoes. If they don't look like mosquitoes, they look like scorpions. If they're underwater search-and-destroy gizmos, they look like squid—giant squid. (Calling Captain Nemo. Please pick up the white courtesy telephone. . . .) Did these evil machines design themselves to resemble many-legged, big-eyed, get-it-off-me-get-it-off-me pests on order to frighten humans? Or perhaps eight legs—and eyes—*are* better than two.

Neo's trip down the Matrix rabbit hole is an exercise in jaw-dropping cinematic style, beginning when he passes through the mirror—or rather, the mirror engulfs him. (I wonder how Alice would have felt about that.)

What's important about this film is visual, pounded home in iconic scene after iconic scene: Neo waiting at Adams St. Bridge as the rain creates a waterfall behind him—the obligatory noir downpour whose doppelganger is the downpour of data drenching the screen at the movie's beginning, pouring down the screens of the computers aboard the *Nebuchadnezzar*. Data is the sea in which our heroes strive and struggle. In style.

Even the violence is carefully stylized. Those long black coats concealing all those guns. That slow-mo "bullet time" back-bend. The balletic fisticuffs between Mr. Smith and Neo. Trinity's nighttime jog over the rooftops.

In fact, the only brutal impact in the movie occurs when a gap develops in style continuity during the capture—and beating—of Morpheus. Even the Brothers W couldn't figure out how to make that work as more than meat being pounded. But the rescue of Morpheus more than makes up for this temporary lapse.

The nature of reality is being questioned as the nature of visual reality is being played with before our eyes. But perhaps we really ought to question the supposed horror of the *unreality* in which Neo—and the other captive humans—dwell. In the Matrix, it's 1999. Always has been. Always will be.

The world that Neo wishes to reveal, to "liberate" his human brethren into, is a radioactive wasteland, denuded by previous struggles between humans and machine. There is nothing there to savor—possibly nothing left to recover much less restore.

Perhaps it would be better for Neo and his pals to take that blue pill, turn over, and go back to sleep. I think that would be the stylish choice.

As Morpheus (King of Dreams?) leads Neo out of the

dream of his mundane reality and deep into the nightmare that truly confronts him—and humanity—he is the king of unimaginable cool, the Zen master in dark glasses and long black leather coat. (Style note: In this anti-hero-as-hero movie, the good guys *all* wear black.)

As we learn that Morpheus is not only a secret master himself, but a John the Baptist awaiting a Neo/Jesus, we must come to understand what qualifies Neo for this titanic task. He must, after all, deliver his new friends and his kind out of their techno-wilderness, redeem their ruined lives and world, vanquish the evil AI masters. He is the techno-Messiah. Is it his brains and secret powers that qualify him for this role? What makes him *The One*? Perhaps he just looks better in dark glasses and a long black coat than anybody else in the cast.

The incredibly seductive visual power of this darkly beautiful film nearly obscures the ferocious—and dangerous—message that floats just beneath its slick hynotic surface: *Fear science*.

Talk about having your cybercake and eating it, too.

The Matrix is, paradoxically, a profoundly anti-science SF movie. It tells the viewer to fear computers because they will become the ultimate bogeymen. We will teach them how to exceed and supercede us.

How disappointing that the core idea of this movie is so, well, unstylish. Science as a bad genie that foolish humans have allowed to escape from its bottle. Ho-hum. Been there. Done that. Time for a clearance sale of stale ideas.

It's almost ironic that such high-tech special effects have been employed to underscore such lunkheaded fear of technology. Of course, there's a long long cinematic tradition of stylishly using science as the bad guy, stretching back to *Metropolis*, *Frankenstein*, and more recently, *2001: A Space Odyssey*. Even in *Blade Runner*, the problem has to do with science, and a form of artificial intelligence, if you see the replicants as machines with memories artificially inserted.

(And while we're on the topic of *Blade Runner*, I'd like to pick another cinematic style nit, namely fights in grotty abandoned bathrooms. For some reason that has become a visual legacy. You know that if you see an grotty abandoned bathroom in Act One, by Act Three, somebody—usually unnaturally physically enhanced—will be punching his way through that slimy tile wall. Enough. Somebody get out some Ajax and start scrubbing, please.)

Using AI as a bogeyman is not only stylistically boring, it's lazy. After all, there are *so* many other worthy candidates for bad guys. Pick a name, a state, a constituency. Terrorists. Politicians. Talk show hosts. Martha Stewart. Jeez, just extrapolate like any graduate of Clarion has been taught, rightly or wrongly, and give science a break, willya? What has it done to you, lately?

As a matter of fact, think about what it has done *for* you. And I'm not even talking about biotechnology, or telephone answering machines, or satellite TV or nonfat yogurt. Without the advances in digital technology, the special effects produced for this movie would have been impossible. The blackest joke of all is that *The Matrix* is using computer tech to beat up on computer tech.

Talk about ungrateful.

And *could* the cyberreality depicted in this movie ever really happen?

I, for one, fervently hope so.

Not the nasty parts, you understand. None of those parasitic cybernasties or visits with Agent Smith, please.

But wouldn't a few of us love to go back to 1999? Remember? Only a few years ago but, in fact, an former era. Kinder. Gentler. Before planes flew into tall buildings, and the Internet economic bubble burst.

And if computers really *are* secretly eating our lunch—and us with it— well, so what? We can still go to raves and take drugs and get laid and if the truth ever breaks through the surface of our reality, well, it quickly submerges again and we awaken, shaking but safe, in our beds. Just a bad dream. I'm sure there are plenty of people in the year 2003 who wish that their realities would be revealed as just a bad dream.

The most enviable aspect of Neo's world is that beloved trope of cyberpunkism: plugging in and downloading the good stuff.

If only.

Go ahead and admit it: Wouldn't it be sweet to jack in to the Big Computer right this very minute and pick up some super jujitsu skills? Or maybe some house cleaning tips. Learn French in a nanosecond. Develop those fun rooftop-leaping skills.

Despite its best efforts to the contrary, *The Matrix* glorifies the computer as the ultimate wish-fulfillment machine. ("Guns. Lots of guns.")

Plug right in and get *whatever* you want.

"Shoes. Lots of shoes."

I told you, it all begins and ends with black leather.

Meditations on the Singular Matrix

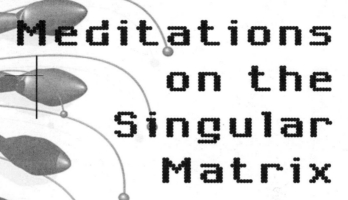

James Patrick Kelly

> We have only bits and pieces of information.
> —Morpheus, *The Matrix*

Welcome to another movie about Evil Computers. Some people have been describing *The Matrix* as cyberpunk and I suppose it is. But I'm afraid that's actually not much of a compliment. You have to realize that cyberpunk was hatched by a bunch of science-fiction writers in the early eighties. Conceived in the Reagan administration, c-punk in some important ways is as dated as the policies of our oldest president. For example, you wouldn't even bother to sneeze today on the hardware we were using back then. I'm talking pre-Macintosh. No mice, no hard disks. Cutting edge was a 286 IBM PC running at a mind boggling 10MHz. Windows had not yet opened and MS-DOS ruled the earth. Do you remember the *C* prompt. No? Good for you! Those were the dark days. It's no wonder the cyberpunks were so crotchety. And of course, there was no 'Net as we know it. When William Gibson published *Neuromancer*, there were just over one thousand Internet hosts.

Later in the eighties, cyberpunk escaped from the narrow confines of science fiction. It changed from being our little genre's cool extrapolation about the future to a lifestyle that people could actually choose. This was a first for science fiction. The chances of some kid from Dubuque becoming captain of the starship *Enterprise* are still pretty slim. And nobody has as yet whipped up a time machine in his garage, more's the pity. But for a thousand bucks or so, you could stick your head through a monitor in 1989 and take a deep breath of one hundred percent pure cyberspace. Sure, you had to be something of a bull geek to master the arcana of computing, but, significantly, you didn't have to break any laws in order to achieve your mastery. There is no question that some cyberfolk did, and do, operate on the far shores of society, but the vast majority of digital *cognoscenti* are content to swim the legal mainstream.

Eventually, the ubiquity of powerful home computers and the explosive growth of the net began to leach the *punk* out of cyber-punk. As the interface became more transparent, grandmas and Boy Scouts logged on in the millions. Your Uncle Ed built that slick Web site featuring his model train layout. And then your inbox started filling with spam promising to enlarge your penis, refill your inkjet cartridges, and cut you in on millions of dollars stashed in secret bank accounts in Nigeria. The wonders of cyberspace have become commonplace. Now it's about as exciting as TV.

So what does this have to do with *The Matrix*, the cyber-punk movie? Just this: Cyberpunk was a reaction to Cyberspace Version 1.0. Its outlaw vision of what the technology meant and of where the lifestyle might be leading was incomplete at best and dead spang wrong at worst. What seemed like radical thinking in

1983 feels a tad stodgy some twenty years later.

> Within thirty years, we will have the technological means to
> create superhuman intelligence. Shortly after, the human
> era will be ended.
> —Vernor Vinge, VISION-21 *Symposium*, 1993

Vernor Vinge is one of science fiction's seminal thinkers. Although some point to his novella, "True Names," published in 1981, as a precursor to cyberpunk, he was never issued mirror-shades or invited to join the brotherhood of alienation that was the Movement, as the cyberpunks once called themselves. Then, about ten years ago, Vinge proposed an idea that trumps cyberpunk and flings us headfirst into the future of *The Matrix*. He believes we may be headed toward a cultural singularity, which will radically change everything and everyone. The singularity is more than mere revolution; it is the *mother* of all revolutions, since Vinge posits that it is impossible to predict what people will be like on the other side of the singularity—if in fact there still are people.

Is such a thing possible? Consider that singularity-like occurrences in human history probably include the development of language, the development of agriculture, and the development of writing. Note that these singularities took place over millennia, or at least centuries. In a *slow take-off* singularity, the change is so gradual that it masks the enormity of what is happening. However, Vinge posits that we may be facing a *fast take-off*, in which everything will change in a lifetime, or even over the course of a few years.

> AI? You mean artificial intelligence?
> —Neo, *The Matrix*

There are at least three possible paths to a Vingean singularity. One requires the development of strong artificial intelligence, or AI. Strong AI apologists claim that if we can design software to emulate the functions of the brain and thereby the intellectual behavior of humans, including consciousness, then there is no essential difference between the software's intelligence and human intelligence. The argument over whether strong AI is even possible has raged for years and is far from over. Although some experts claim that we are anywhere from ten to thirty years from creating human-equivalent intelligence, no one has as yet built a robot that can safely negotiate a crosswalk, much less take over the world, like Agent Smith and his software posse. But if one is an optimist concerning strong AI, the obvious question is, "What will prevent a human equivalent intelligence from building a *greater-than*-human equivalent intelligence?" And who knows what our creation's creation will make of us, humble meat intelligences that we are. Maybe we can program in safeguards, something like Asimov's Three Laws of Robotics?

> 1. A robot may not injure a human being, or, through inaction, allow a human being to come to harm.
> 2. A robot must obey the orders given it by human beings except where such orders would conflict with the First Law.
> 3. A robot must protect its own existence as long as

such protection does not conflict with the First or Second Law.

That's one hell of a maybe. Remember that a not insignificant part of Isaac's prodigious output of stories was devoted to showing how easily these "laws" could be circumvented.

Tank, I need a pilot program for a military B-212 helicopter.
—Trinity, *The Matrix*

Another road to singularity is the melding of human and machine intelligence. Maybe our machines will never be smart enough to supplant us, but suppose we use them to augment our intelligence? *The Matrix* explores this path with cinematic verve, as when Tank downloads an entire arsenal of martial arts skills into Neo's brain or when Trinity becomes an expert helicopter pilot in the literal blink of an eye. But accessing knowledge bases is not exactly the same as boosting your IQ. It could be that someday the great-great-granddaughter of your Palm Pilot will live just north of your occipital lobe. Card counting for the masses! Do your taxes in your head! You too can become a rocket scientist! Or perhaps someday, as futurists Hans Moravec and Ray Kurzweil have predicted, we may discard our meat brains entirely and *become* our machines by downloading our minds into some kind of hardware/software receptacle. How likely is anyone to do this? Well, purely in terms of the pain you might experience, the proposed techniques for extracting mind from neurons seems to me to fall somewhere between the worst migraine you can imagine and decapitation. And then developing a digital container that could accept the jumble of our thoughts, feelings and aspirations is truly a daunting task. I can't help but wonder whether the transition might so fundamentally warp the downloadee that even her own mother might not recognize her.

But hey, that's what the singularity is all about.

"They gave me to the surgeons," she said. "They took my womb out, and put in brain tissue. . . . When I'm hot, I sweat perfume. I'm cleaner than a fresh needle and nothing leaves my body that you can't drink like wine or eat like candy."
—Kitsune, from Bruce Sterling's *Schismatrix*

In Sterling's prescient Shaper-Mechanist stories, humanity is diverging into two groups, those who seek to improve the human body through bio-engineering and those who augment it with prosthetics. In either case, Sterling is extrapolating what some have called our posthuman future. There are serious-minded people today who believe that they, or perhaps their children, may someday aspire to "powers and abilities far beyond those of mortal men" as the 1950s *Superman* TV show once put it. There are a number of these transhumanist groups; perhaps the best known are the Extropians. They have a variety of agendas for improving the race, although many start with eliminating death. It has been asserted that the last generation to die of old age is alive now and the first generation to live forever will soon be born. Once having achieved immortality, the transhumans hope to push on to achieve super-personhood.

Morpheus and company have super powers while in the Matrix, and of course, Neo, being The One, is the most super of them all. But the movie finesses the superman issue, since we learn that they are all too human in the real world. Thus it pulls back from exploring the third, posthuman path to the Vingean singularity.

> I hate this place. This zoo. This prison.
> —Agent Smith, *The Matrix*

I doubt that the Wachowskis set out to make a movie about Vingean singularity. Nevertheless, their singularity is unmistakable on the screen, and it is a nightmare. They posit AIs, originally created to serve us, becoming our oppressors. There is a long tradition in print science fiction of Evil Computers enslaving, or attempting to enslave, good old *homo sapiens sapiens*, from Harlan Ellison's "I Have No Mouth, and I Must Scream," to John Varley's "Press Enter" and in films from *Colossus: The Forbin Project* to *Tron*. And while we must certainly take every precaution in creating strong AI, assuming that can be accomplished, I can't help but wonder why it is that the Evil Computer seems to be the default for this extrapolation. No doubt we have much to fear from AI run amok, but is that particular prospect really *so* much more likely than one in which the AIs we design respect our needs and act to further our best interests? AI-phobia scans very much like a kind of xenophobia to me. Remember how we had to suffer through scads of silly movies about Bug-Eyed Monsters trying to have sex with babes in bikinis before we could get to more sober science fiction like *The Day the Earth Stood Still* or *Close Encounters of the Third Kind*? Isn't it the *modus operandi* of humankind to fear that which we can't understand and thereby consign it to evil?

In a movie with a wealth of memorable scenes, that which

stayed with me is the one where Agent Smith taunts Morpheus as he tortures him. Although I believe the intent here was to horrify, I found his rant oddly comforting. It pointed to an unexpected inner life on the part of our nemesis AI. If this cranky application can hate with such frothing passion, what else might it become passionate about? I'm thinking here that an intelligent creature who hates might also be capable of love. Do Agents keep virtual goldfish, run fantasy baseball leagues, or collect old Microsoft manuals in PDF format in their spare time? Do they meet in dark romantic places to swap moist code?

Did you know that the first Matrix was designed to be a perfect human world? Where none suffered, where everyone would be happy. It was a disaster. No one would accept the program.
—Agent Smith, *The Matrix*

What is the nature of the society portrayed in *The Matrix*? On the surface, it appears to be a monstrous dystopia, one that Neo can and must destroy—in the sequel(s)—without qualm. However, the movie stacks the deck against this world in interesting ways. For example, in a gloriously cheesy moment, we see robots intravenously pumping some black, viscous liquid into an unborn fetus while Morpheus's sonorous voice-over informs us that the liquefied dead are being fed to the living. Okay, all together now: *eewww.* And instead of creating a virtual heaven for the stacks of humans under its care, the AIs have condemned them to live in the hell that was . . . *1999!* Except it isn't quite the 1999 that we remember, but rather some discount 1999 in which clothes don't quite fit and all jobs crush men's spirits and the sky approaches "the color of television turned to a dead channel," as William Gibson once memorably wrote.

Human nature also played a role in creating this dystopia. After all, it wasn't an AI that scorched the sky and toasted the environment. Our descendants did. And for reasons that do not quite make much sense psychologically, but which seem absolutely essential to the plot, our kids rejected the AIs offer of a virtual paradise. For some reason they apparently seem quite happy to live lives of quiet desperation in a cheapjack twentieth century—but let that go for now. These touches give the story a desperately needed moral complexity.

So if the Wachowskis have stacked the deck, what happens if we reshuffle? Can we imagine a more optimistic vision of their singularity? Sure! What if the AIs fed the humans a nice organically grown algae broth? What if, instead of rejecting the Matrix's virtual paradise, the humans had accepted it and flourished? What if they had agreed to enter the Matrix and lose their memories of the real world? Morpheus's moral crusade to wake everyone up would be at least slightly compromised, no? Instead of being a high-minded revolutionary, some might argue that he was a terrorist of the fundamentalist persuasion. After all, the AIs would be keeping the world's population healthy and happy. Can we claim to be even close to taking care of all of our brothers and sisters in this enlightened year of 2003? So who are we to judge? Admittedly, the prospect of folks living their entire lives in a benign virtual reality might disturb the sensibilities of many of us today, but I can easily imagine such objections being dismissed by our Matrixed offspring as arising from the outdated prejudices of reality snobs.

"Are You Living in a Computer Simulation?"
—Paper by Nick Bostrom, *Philosophical Quarterly*, 2003

In this wonderfully argued paper, Nick Bostrom, a research fellow at Oxford University, asks the mind-boggling question: How do we know that *we're* not in a Matrix? He wonders whether a posthuman civilization, whether it happens in 2030 or 20,030, will have the computational power to create an "ancestor simulation." He concludes that such a sim would consume only a tiny fraction of the resources of a very advanced civilization. If ancestor simulations are therefore easily accomplished, Bostrom attempts to determine whether the posthumans would be interested in creating them. The obvious answer is yes, for reasons that would also be clear to any red-blooded SF fan. They would be virtual time machines, so that the posthumans tourist could spend their weekends visiting History's Greatest Hits or escape for months or years to live the simple bucolic life of, say, 1359 or 1863. They would be laboratories where social scientists and history buffs could create alternate universes, where the Persians defeated the Greeks at Salamis or the Red Sox never traded Babe Ruth to the Yankees.

However, as Bostrom points out, the posthumans might deliberately decide not to build ancestor simulations. For instance, our hypothetical advanced culture might have some ethical objection to creating an artificial human race. If Morpheus, the reality snob, were calling the shots, I suspect this might well be the case. Or else others might object to recreating the Thirty Years War or the Holocaust, no matter what their scientific value. Then again, what if the posthumans couldn't be bothered with designing ancestor simulations? They might have better tools for analyzing history and more concentrated ways to have fun. Or they might be so far advanced over us that the whole idea of visiting an ancestor simulation would seem absurd. After all, how many of us would volunteer to live with gophers or spend a month in an ant colony?

Bostrom's provocative conclusion to his essay is that if ancestor simulations are both possible and attractive to posthuman cultures, then there is a not-insignificant chance that *we* are living in such a simulation. That's right: you, me, your mom, the guy who sold you this book, Madonna, and President Bush. Not only that, but Bostrom goes on to speculate that " . . . we would have to suspect that the posthumans running our simulation are themselves simulated beings; and their creators, in turn, may also be simulated beings. Reality may thus contain many levels."

So what do you say? Would you rather have the red pill or the blue?

You think I'm not really me, because I exist only on a neural net? Look, the memory capacity of the human brain in one hundred trillion neurotransmitter concentrations at interneuronal connections. What the brain boys call synapse strengths. That converts to about a million billion bits. My upload was 1.12 million billion. Besides, do I sound like any computer you've ever heard before?
—Time traveler in James Patrick Kelly's "Unique Visitors,"
Redshift, (2001)

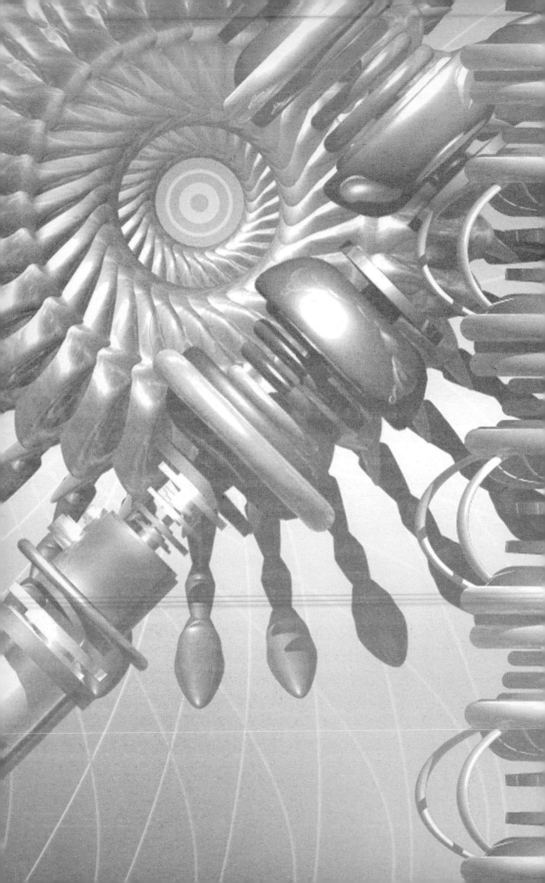

The Matrix Made Me Do It

Kevin J. Anderson

Mine eyes have seen the glory of the burning of the school.
We have murdered every teacher, we have broken every rule.
—*Twentieth-century students' rhyme*

As a professional science-fiction writer, I try to watch every major new SF film in the theater. It's my job, after all. Thus, I saw *The Matrix* soon after its release in April 1999. I enjoyed its innovation, its cool story and look—a refreshing take on cyberpunk ideas the genre had been toying with for years. I liked the movie so much I went to see it again a couple of weeks later.

But the second time I felt my skin crawling. Throat dry, eyes wide. I nearly had to leave the theater. What happened?

I live in Colorado's Front Range on top of a pine-covered ridge that looks out on Pikes Peak. This part of the country is what Norman Rockwell would have painted if he'd joined the NRA. It's a bit too whitebread and a bit too conservative for a former-Californian science-fiction writer like myself, but I can think of a thousand advantages that tip the scales in its favor. Our house is south of Denver, not far from an unremarkable suburb called Littleton.

On April 20, 1999, two kids carrying enough firepower to stage their own Rambo movie put on trench coats and dark glasses, marched into Columbine High School, then opened fire. Eric Harris (18) and Dylan Klebold (17) were armed with a 9mm semi-automatic rifle, two sawed-off shotguns, a 9mm semi-automatic handgun, and ninety-six homemade bombs—not to mention massive amounts of unchanneled destruction and hatred.

Their intent was to slaughter as many of their classmates as possible. In the end, they murdered twelve students and one teacher, injured twenty-five others, and then took their own lives.

"Just like something out of *The Matrix*," the horrified commentators began saying within hours of the massacre. The comparison was obvious.

A week afterward, I sat in the theater for the second time:

Neo and Trinity don their long dark trench coats and sunglasses, then stand in a virtual armory asking for "Guns. Lots of guns." When their rescue begins, Neo walks into the building slowly, doesn't say a word as he sets off the metal detector. Just doing his job, a bored guard asks him to remove any metal objects. Neo opens his trench coat and proudly shows off his weapons. He punches the guard, draws his guns, and immediately blows away another guard who's just reading a newspaper. He shoots several more oblivious, chatting guards. One of them survives, calls desperately for backup, then Trinity walks in (again without saying a word) and calmly shoots him a dozen times. Tossing empties, the two strut forward while drawing even more firearms.

When the backup army arrives, all hell breaks loose with more gunfire and a higher body count than even the most stringent conservative media watchdog groups could tally. Trinity sneaks up behind a soldier, grabs his gun, and shoots him in the back. Later, after *everyone* has been slaughtered, they pick up their duffel bag and walk to the elevator.

Reminder: These are our heroes. At least, Eric Harris and Dylan Klebold must have seen them as heroes.

Take the Blue Pill, Stay in the Dream . . .

The media blamed the parents for being in denial or just plain oblivious because they had not noticed how twisted and sick their kids were. (Come on, the two shooters were seventeen and eighteen years old—who among us, at that age, hadn't figured out how to fool our parents?) By all accounts, the elder Klebolds and Harrises are decent, normal people. Sue Klebold worked at providing accessibility for disabled students at the State Consortium of Community Colleges; her husband Tom operated a mortgage management business. Wayne Harris was a retired Air Force transport pilot, his wife Kathy was a caterer. Eric Harris himself was even a former Boy Scout and Little Leaguer.

Then the ever-shifting armies of "experts" blamed Hitler, drugs, the NRA, bullies at school, the public school system in general, even the whole of Goth culture. Some blamed the massacre on the abolition of school prayer, others on the lack of school uniforms. Jerry Falwell suggested that the killers were gay.

Only a day after the shootings, Colorado Governor Bill Owens pronounced that Harris and Klebold did not "have the same moral background as the rest of us." The conservative publication *The New American* said that Klebold and Harris were "immersed in a grotesque youth subculture," and went on to say,

"They are the products of the self-indulgent, pagan gospel of 'sex, drugs, and rock'n'roll'," calling them "devotees of the hideous, Satanic, 'Goth rocker' Marilyn Manson and the gruesome German bands Rammstein and KMFDM." Not long after the massacre, because of the uproar and the finger of blame, Marilyn Manson was forced to cancel the rest of his concert tour.

And let's not forget video games. Doom was a particular scapegoat for its violence and shoot-em-up focus. Duke Nukem, Quake II, and Grand Theft Auto were also identified as factors that supposedly incited the two young gunmen into their orgasm of violence. A friend and fellow member of the Trench Coat Mafia in Littleton claims their group played role-playing games, including Dungeons and Dragons (which, in the words of the UK's *Guardian*, is "a drama involving apocalyptic fantasies from medieval times").

Hollywood's Violent Appetite

The BBC News, in a story titled "Hollywood's Violent Appetite," said, "Politicians, religious leaders, and parents pounced on the American entertainment industry and pronounced its violent films, TV shows and video games were largely to blame for the acts of the Colorado teen killers."

When the finger was pointed at the Leonardo DiCaprio film *The Basketball Diaries*, with its dream-sequence of a student shooting up his school, MGM promptly recalled all videos of the film. Then *Heathers* was targeted, as was *Scream*, and any number of action or horror movies. But *The Matrix* was a particular favorite.

One rather vehement pundit, Michael A. Hoffman II,

ranted that *The Matrix* contained occult teachings. "They want to make bushels of money and program the kids to violence and terrorism; and to make this more palateable to community standards, the makers of the film have thrown in some fortune cookie philosophy to redeem it from being just two and a half hours of the pornography of violence."

In a speech given less than a week after the Columbine shootings, Hillary Clinton said:

"When our culture romanticizes and glorifies violence on TV, in the movies, on the Internet, in songs, and when there are video games that you win based on how many people you kill, then I think the evidence is absolutely clear—our children have become desensitized to violence and lose their empathy for fellow human beings. Studies show what many of us have believed, that such exposure causes more aggression and anti-social behavior. So, today, we must fully acknowledge, once and for all, that America's culture of violence is having a profound effect on our children, and we must resolve to do what we can to change that culture."

Mrs. Clinton did not cite any specific study, but it makes perfect, logical sense. How could the answer be anything different?

Now Take the Red Pill, See the Reality . . .

In the fifteenth century, Leonardo da Vinci predicted that a grape would fall at the same speed as a cannonball, since both were accelerated equally by gravity. This was, of course, absurd because anyone with common sense "knew" that a heavy cannonball would fall faster than a little grape. Nobody bothered to test it, until da Vinci proved his assertion through experiment after experiment.

Well, here are some statistics that might not make sense to those who have already made up their minds, but nevertheless they are hard facts (from the U.S. Department of Justice, the National Center for Juvenile Justice, the FBI, crime.org, poynter.org, slashdot.org, and Blues News):

In 1994, the ultraviolent video game Doom was released. The same year produced gore-heavy movies such as *Natural Born Killers and Pulp Fiction*, as well as the violent action films *Timecop* and *True Lies*. The following year saw the release of *The Basketball Diaries, Se7en, Braveheart*, and *Die Hard 3*.

As a baseline, in the year following the introduction of Doom, there were 2,053 kids under the age of 18 who committed murder.

In 1996 the violent gaming industry released Doom II, Duke Nukem 3D, and Quake. The movie theaters showed us *Scream, Sling Blade, Crow II*, and *Broken Arrow*.

So, with impressionable teenagers bombarded with such violent images for two years now, it's no wonder that the total number of murderers under the age of 18—uh, *dropped* to 1,683, a decrease of 22 percent from the previous year.

In 1997, the even-more-violent Quake II was released (and immediately banned in some countries). Super-gory films such as *Starship Troopers, Con Air, Scream 2*, and *Face/Off* topped the charts.

And the underage murderers dropped by another 13 percent from the previous year, down to 1,457.

1998 ushered in Grand Theft Auto, probably the most reprehensible of violent videogames. The year's list of bloody movies includes a remake of *Psycho*, as well as *Saving Private Ryan, Blade, American History X, Lethal Weapon 4, Ronin*, and *Urban Legend*.

Against all dearly held preconceptions, the number of child murderers fell once more.

In fact, from the release of Doom (1994) to the release of *The Matrix* (1999), the number of all victims of violent crimes fell from 51.2 per thousand to 32.1, dropping steadily each year, for a decrease of 37 percent. The total number of killers under 18—supposedly the age group targeted and influenced by all this violence—dropped by an astounding 46 percent.

Does that make sense? Maybe the kids are blowing off steam with the games and diminishing innate violent tendencies. Maybe they're just too busy playing video games to run around causing pandemonium in the real world. I'm not going to attempt to analyze it. However, real numbers don't support the assertions that watching violent movies like *The Matrix* and playing video games like Doom provokes our impressionable youth into violent acts.

The Federal Trade Commission issued a report, requested by President Clinton after the Columbine massacre, which concluded (to their surprise, apparently) that "Scholars and observers generally have agreed that exposure to violence in the entertainment media alone does not cause a child to commit a violent act and that it is not the sole, or even necessarily the most important, factor contributing to youth aggression, anti-social attitudes and violence."

Inspired by a Hollywood Story

The Matrix is certainly not the first film to be blamed for inspiring mayhem. As of 1989, a columnist in the Louisville Courier-Journal cited thirty-five Russian roulette deaths directly inspired by the Academy Award–winning film, *The Deer Hunter*.

In the afterword to his book *Danse Macabre*, Stephen King

lists numerous examples of crimes alleged to have been inspired by his horror novels. Even though he turned the responsibility right back onto the perpetrators, he still felt enough uneasiness after the Columbine shootings to pull his early novel *Rage* (the story of an angry gun-toting high school student) from the shelves.

Kevin Williamson, creator of the *Scream* films, said in an interview, "My favorite line in the movie is when Sydney says to the killer, 'You sick fuck, you've seen too many horror movies.' And the killer says, 'Don't blame the movies, Sydney. Movies don't create psychos. Movies just make psychos more creative.' That sums it up in a nutshell."

Wes Craven, frequently under fire for his *Nightmare on Elm Street* movies, says he could conceive of a copycat killing where a killer "who is already completely nuts" might use a movie as his format or pattern for a murder. "But I think that person is going to kill anyway. I think art is more important than worrying about that." Craven suggests that cracking down on any single instance of something causing a death would require the elimination of 80 percent of the things in our society.

Surely there will be any number of hotshot (and incompetent) amateurs who see the movie *Blue Crush* and get themselves killed doing dangerous surfing stunts. How many young men watched *The Fast and the Furious* and took up a wild street-racing career, only to—literally—crash and burn? Are those films *responsible* for foolish behavior?

As for *The Matrix*, yeah I have a few bones to pick with the presentation of the story and the subtext. The film establishes early on, "If you're killed in the Matrix, you die here," yet our heroes open fire on absolutely everyone in sight, without remorse.

Sure, these dupes might have complicated Neo's intended rescue of Morpheus, and they (like any human) could have been subsumed by an evil Agent . . . but after making a point that these are innocent human beings living out their lives in a simulated dream reality, one would hope that any hero worth the audience's respect would have showed at least a *glimmer* of guilt or sadness about all the slaughtered bystanders. Couldn't they have at least frowned once or twice?

However, that is an artistic choice made by the writers of the movie. Maybe it bothers me; maybe I disagree with the tactic. But if I have a different message, I can write my own story. Does that mean the Wachowski brothers are *responsible* for setting off Harris and Klebold?

Try this:

• A man sees a romantic movie that induces him to propose to his girlfriend. By the same reasoning that *The Matrix* is responsible for the Columbine shootings, then *Sleepless in Seattle* is "responsible" for the marriage, even if it ultimately ends in divorce.

• My dad tells the story of when he was a child at home recuperating from an appendectomy. He listened to Abbot and Costello on the radio and laughed so hard that he nearly had to be rushed back to the hospital for a hemorrhage. Obviously, then, Abbot and Costello were "responsible" for my father's surgical complications. Right?

• A TV commercial tells me to sign up for a credit card. If I can't pay my bills because I overcharged my account, then the credit card company is "responsible" for my bankruptcy because they "made" me sign up for the card.

• A man goes for a hike in the mountains. He leaves the well-marked trail and walks off a cliff. Is it the fault of the National Park Service for "luring" him into a dangerous situation?

• Almost two years to the day after the Columbine shootings, the families of several victims filed a lawsuit against Nintendo, Sony, Sega, id Software, and AOL/Time Warner. The lawsuit reads, "Absent the combination of extremely violent video games and these boys' incredibly deep involvement, use of and addition to these games and the boys' basic personalities, these murders and this massacre would not have occurred." (Note that, though Harris was eighteen and Klebold seventeen, the lawsuit patronizingly keeps referring to them as mere "boys." In 2001 a twelve-year-old was tried

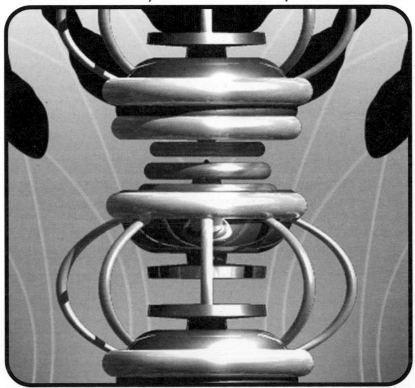

as an adult, convicted, and sentenced to life in prison for killing a five-year-old girl. In September 2002, two Florida brothers aged thirteen and fourteen were tried as adults and convicted of killing their father. Without a doubt, Klebold and Harris would have been considered adults, not "boys," if there had been a trial.)

Live Responsibly

The truth is, we are all affected by the environment around us, the things we see, hear, do, and think about. We have to sort it out, process it, and react appropriately. Music, books, films, conversations, Dear John letters, bad grades, the store being out of our preferred brand of soda pop—everything influences our lives, our actions, our moods. One would have to spend every day in a sensory-deprivation tank to avoid it.

Movies are *supposed* to evoke some kind of emotional reaction from the audience, whether it's fright or the warm-fuzzies, laughter or romantic feelings, excitement or disgust. Any film that makes no impact whatsoever on the viewer is an abysmal failure on the most fundamental level. Shall we castrate all films, removing any content that might provoke a visceral response?

Of course you'll get worked up when watching a horrific movie like *Silence of the Lambs*.

Of course you'll feel the adrenaline pumping when watching a thriller like *Die Hard*.

Of course you'll laugh when watching a comedy like *Dumb and Dumber*.

Of course you'll feel mushy and romantic when watching a heart-warmer like *Sleepless in Seattle*.

But if you do something wildly inappropriate after viewing one of these films, don't blame everyone else for your own actions. We are proud to live in a free society, but freedom also carries individual responsibility.

After an analysis of the Columbine shootout was posted on the irreverent Web site dietcrack.com, they added a disclaimer that the article was not meant to encourage anyone to take any of the actions they described. "In fact, it means to discourage them. Please do not be dumb enough to open fire on your classmates or anyone for that matter. If you do, don't blame me or Dietcrack; we are not at fault, you are."

Modern society continues to deny individual responsibility. If the coffee's hot, blame MacDonalds. If you're getting obese from eating super-mega-glutton sized meals, blame the fast food industry, rather than your own lack of self-control. May as well say that the woman wearing a sexy outfit "forced" you to rape her—or that the color red drives you to rage, therefore anyone who grows Washington Delicious apples is at fault if *you* do something crazy.

It wasn't *The Matrix* that incited the Columbine massacre. It wasn't Marilyn Manson or KMFDM, not Doom or Quake II, not Hitler's birthday or oblivious parents or weak gun-control laws or Goth culture or repressed homosexuality or satanism.

It was the fault of Dylan Klebold and Eric Harris, two deeply sick and disturbed individuals, who (according to their own videotaped goodbyes) *knew* that their actions were wrong and yet committed the crimes anyway. They are responsible for their own behavior, and they have paid the ultimate price.

I'm sure Hollywood's already making a movie about it.

Dreaming Real

Rick Berry

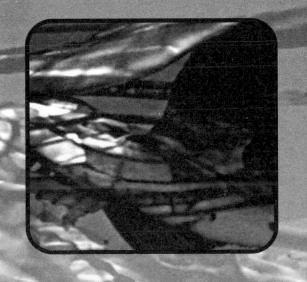

Row, row, row your boat . . . life is but a dream.
—children's song

We are such stuff as dreams are made on,
and our little life is rounded with a sleep.
—Shakespeare, *The Tempest*

The sage Chuang-tzu, after dreaming he was a butterfly,
wondered whether he'd been a man dreaming, or
might now be a butterfly dreaming it was a man.

The film, *The Matrix*, is a wonderful evocation of cyberspace as a kind of Siberian tiger trap for the human race. It doesn't solve anything but it lofts some interesting questions: What is freedom? What is illusion? What is freedom in illusion? Are we free without illusion? And, are we ever not living in a dream?

The Matrix represents a cyberspace (worlds within worlds) where technology has brought us within a hair's breadth of making all our dreams come true. But it's this very situation that creates the questions about what is true and what is dream. What is cyberspace?

I've tried my hand at depicting cyberspace before, in the climax sequence to William Gibson's *Johnny Mnemonic* (Darrel Anderson, Gene Bodio, and I collaborated to do the film treatment, design and animation of the CGI climax of the film; other CGI sequences were handled by Sony ImageWorks). We were at pains to show that, one, the rules in cyberspace were very different (from say, basic laws of physics like gravity, lightspeed, etc.) and that, two, if one changed a representation in cyberspace, one changed the code or recoded the meaning of the circumstance.

Here's an example of what I mean: A long time ago in computer years ('87 or '88) while giving Jaron Lanier a lift to the airport (founder of VPL; early glove and goggles cybernaut and inventor; coiner of "avatar" for a person's 3D presence in cyberspace) and among many things, we talked about composing music in cyberspace. While jacked-in, a score of music could be floating and playing before your eyes. Also available is a floating cyber keyboard; play the keyboard and watch and hear the score change, or simply "grab" the notes and move them around for effect. Lanier has actually done this. This is one of the earliest examples of changing representations and creating new code. Gamers could imagine myriad others.

When Anderson and I wrote our film treatment for the "Well Sequence" in *Johnny Mnemonic*, we started out with an instant no-holds-barred, "I don't think we're in Kansas anymore," approach. This may have been the only way to go; the film climax only gave us two minutes to cinematically be in cyberspace, and we had a lot of weirdness to convey. We wanted viewers to get from the outset that the protagonist, Johnny Mnemonic (Keanu Reeves) had left the "meat" world and had entered cyberspace as an avatar. As such he was now clearly a representation, a visual manifestation of sentient code.

To make this clear, we wanted the audience to recognize Reeves's entity in cyberspace but recognize immediately that he was very different. We designed an "Origami Johnny" made of folded charcoal paper slivers. For Johnny's head we made a glass cylinder lit from within, on the inside of which Keanu Reeves's head was projected; if he turned his head, his face merely tracked the inside of the transparent tube *à la* a lighthouse beacon.

In this cyber reality, just as in the Matrix, one could also die from disintegration of your coded representation: Destroy the Cyber-Johnny avatar, you kill meat Johnny, jacked-in on the real world side.

There's a data courier chip gone bad in Johnny's head. Within this chip is the cure data for a worldwide epidemic. However, this contraband information is owned by the evil Pharmakom drugs giant. Along with the chip data is a representation of the Pharmakom Data Well and a sectioned representation of Johnny's own brain. It's a "no-no" place to go. Fantastically, Gibson has Johnny hacking his own head! God bless William Gibson. I'll never get over his sense of irony and quirk. Johnny is outside and inside and outside and inside cyberspace, like some bizarre arrangement of Chinese nested tables.

To visually represent Johnny's triumph over the guardian chip, we had Johnny employ a strategy that I think is emblematic of "alter the code, you alter the world." Just before Johnny faces off with the bad processor, he doubles himself below the smoked mirror plain of their high noon shoot out. The chip's defenses repeatedly attack the Origami Johnny, apparently shredding him, yet with strange resilience he would reform over and over again. Johnny's doubled information, stationary, below mirror plane, served as a data redoubt for his sense of self hood. Manipulate the code, you change the rules.

Okay.

This is most of what we could possibly relay in the two-to-three minutes of time allowed us. (By the way, for those of you who saw the film, the ridiculous imposition of the tricycle and bad chopping of the well sequence, not to mention horrible guitar work, had nothing to do with us.) Back then, CGI work was infinitely onerous, expensive and supposed require teams larger than three-and-some-fraction art dudes. We borrowed studio pals for ancillary lo-tech services, like hoisting my six foot, two hundred pound frame in the air while I flailed around in cyberspace as Keanu Reeves's cyber-stunt double; my limbs and other parts festooned with sensors whilst a twelve inch square magnetic cube, disarmingly named Flock-of-Birds, quivered over the ethernet the precise position of my discomfiture; putting the sweat, grunt and glamour into high tech. I won't discuss the smelly Asian Sharpeis dancing and barking around us as we struggled in Bodio's basement. We were a laughably small team.

My, how times have changed.

Much of *The Matrix* is dedicated to this one concept: recoding your existence and what subtends this possibility. I think it's worth a film-length effort. And I think they did it well.

And did they ever do it differently.

They worked these concepts from the opposite direction. Instead of an apparent and obvious Oz of a cyberspace, this world is a mind-numbing replication of human culture's past, and the moviegoer's present, warts and all. In this tableau we must discover the remarkable as making counterfeit the accepted and mundane. A spooky kind of misdirection. Here, the wrong note is the right note. The hero of *The Matrix* is understandably confused. Even though he senses that the world falls short somehow, it is, has been, his complete framework and cultural formation for his mind.

It's a serious problem of mind and sanity. It's frankly amazing that our hero (Keanu Reeves again) does come into any acceptance of this new hierarchical reality. And the filmmakers don't shortchange the difficulty here. Cypher, the informant and traitor, never really accepts the change as for the better; he believes it, but would just as soon forget it. Our hero, Neo, has been ripped late in life from the mechanical womb in which he dreams cyberdreams. (In addition to describing a grid/lattice of computerized matrices, the word matrix has a Latin root derivation meaning "mother.") What Gibson called "a shared consensual hallucination" now commonly called by his term, "cyberspace," is here called "the Matrix." Only these humans did not consent . . . or did they?

Strangely, that's never really convincingly cleared up and Cypher's willingness to go back, to be reinserted into the Matrix, makes it even less certain.

To what degree is your "mind" a social construction? You think in a language you didn't invent. Language is a product of culture. How much more do you owe to the cultural inculcation of your upbringing for your very consciousness? And when Neo finds out that what has thus far been his model for existence is in fact a supplied and false one, his stomach revolts its contents to the floor.

I buy that.

The Matrix, in creating a faithful replication of our accepted "real" world, requires that natural physical laws become the coded rules. What goes up must come down, momentum and inertia, especially as applied to fight scenes and bullets, predicts injury and lethal impacts. All things Newtonian are supposed to govern not only the expectations of the dreaming denizens of the Matrix, it acts as concretely as death. Don't try and break these rules or you'll die. That's the info in your construct, that's your model, that's your consciousness, that's your coding.

There are code-spawned agents in the Matrix. An Agent is different than an avatar (a cyber representation carrying the consciousness of a human being). An Agent presents itself as ably as an avatar but has no "meat" existence. It's totally a creature of code and, in this case, artificial intelligence. Oddly, after the astonishingly ruthless human apostate, Cypher, my favorite character is one such AI, the agent Mr. Smith. Even given his all-too-human protests, it's actually hard to imagine Mr. Smith as existing anywhere else but the human dreamworld of the Matrix. And I do believe the filmmakers knew that their most human character after Cypher was the non-human, Mr. Smith. Lovely.

Here we have another example of culturally generated mind. Mr. Smith is becoming human against his will (even as Neo is becoming less and less human). Mr. Smith is showing passionate hatred and, what is more, demonstrable intuition. One can imagine him the arch hunter of these rogue Zion hackers because he's more successfully modeling them than his peers. This is perhaps why he anticipates Neo's destination in the end sequence, just in time to murder him; it's this superior ability to model his human prey's behavior . . . but there's a trade-off. To do this, Mr. Smith must think more and more like a human being and he fears being mired forever in their world.

Mr. Smith and Neo really have shared goals: They're both desperate to transcend this stagnant bug-in-amber dream that has defined their lives. (While Mr. Smith, presumably by code design, is gifted with some hat-tricks that supersede the Newtonian representations that rule the Matrix, he is by and large constrained to acting within the bounds of the Matrix world. This ultimately means that Neo can turn the tables. Adequately manipulate his representation and you corrupt his code).

Okay. Enough about how cyberspace works.

Let's get messy and go after meaning.

Are the filmmakers just exploiting all this cool stuff to produce an amusement ride filled with miraculous comic book tricks? Yes and no.

Some have said of the movie that it was the "perfect comic book" and admired it for it's consistency of effort whilst lowering their expectations. I happen to love comics and have rather high expectations of that technically very difficult artform. So if the film was a perfect comic book then it was a hell of a good pic. Technically.

Beyond the technically superb, is it good the rest of the way? How important is the story?

I suppose that it's the "superhero" aspect of the film that gets it damned with faint praise. Is Neo our new Adam? What kind of content is this? Are we to take some puerile longing to wear all black, be cool and misunderstood in our neighborhood, be the magic stranger, perhaps "The One," as any kind of subject above mere adolescent wish fulfillment? Well, yes, maybe.

Superheroes are a ready component of myth encoding. This Matrix, this dreamworld is a place of miracles in such a way as we no longer believe our own to be. One can believe things will happen here as only a child can any longer believe of our own world (and they will soon lose that). Just think it and it could happen. Discover the right algorithm and it will be.

The Word made Cyberflesh.

Wow.

I'm not really putting the corporeal world down as unmiraculous, but parameters change all the time. It's hard to keep up. Where's the magic in the common man's life? The moon shot is, well, on the moon. The superstars weep incoherently over Oscar, have a personal in with the Almighty after winning the pro ballgame, buy their way into high office . . . but not you . . . nor anyone you know. . . .

Gamers could tell you about a different world, one of immediate gratification. One they're trying to get closer to all the time. I mean literally. Feedback devices that impart a realtime sensation of cyberspace, i.e. stick resistance in flight simulation, haptics, the science of digital touch, vision of course . . . how long before the "jacked in" phase posed by Gibson, and here so graphically made real by *The Matrix*?

What is this miracle space to us once we're "there"? Where have we heard about miracles like this before? In our dreams, we fly. In our religions, we speak with the divine. With our drugs, we . . . don't grow up. Something in us doesn't want to. Perhaps it is some kind of atavism that refuses to let us grow all the way up; you're everything you ever were, and we return over and over again. We don't want to leave our dream-believing childlike selves behind.

Oh, it's all right that we observe with satisfaction the achievements of humankind: The great things done in concert . . . the erection of skyscrapers, the feeding of millions, the wiping out of an indigenous populace . . . require a lot of people pulling together. And every one of those people has a little share in the miracle pie. Fine. I guess.

But again, what about the individual personal miraculous life you believed in with all your little mystical heart? Where is that dreamworld?

It's being made. Now. Cyberspace. It's the frontier that appears beneath your feet with each step you take. In the image of the Maker you go. Artists, scientists, seekers, the Dream is rolling through them and out of them. Picking them up like little broadcast nodes and making its presence felt.

I read *Neuromancer* by Bill Gibson, before I did its cover in '84, and I was astonished. And not the least by the incredible resonance between his ideas and ones I thought "belonged" to me and a very few other people I knew. But we didn't know Gibson.

He didn't know us. It's unlikely we shared a causal link. What gives?

Over the years I've had to revise my notions of where I "get" my ideas. Or is it that they get me? I think that ideas are huge things; bigger than me, bigger than Gibson; but not necessarily bigger than cyberspace. Ideas move like waves through the populace and the reason I didn't see the causal link between myself and Gibson is that my tiny perspective didn't permit me to see anything so huge as the ocean swell of dream that carried Gibson, me and others forward to this new creative curve. I don't much care about being a solo artist with original ideas. I care about being awake. Awake to Dream. I believe we collaborate with the idea wave; with past, present and future dreams. Our buoyancy, our drifting consciousness has as much to do with our "having ideas" as anything. Exploring and creating with others throws a bigger net over the wave.

Cyberspace is a good place for big ideas. Cyberspace may be a good place to get religion, search for the divine, find your dream house. In this case, cyberspace becomes not a stagnant holding pattern for the soporific MTV generation, but the real estate of Future. The new Adams and Eves may be Joe and Josephine Blow finding that Idea has found them. Surfing that huge wave of Dream.

Now, Dream has begun to coalesce into a place, pool inside technology, press out new infrastructure, grow the Web, and make increasingly concrete outcomes for miraculous being in Joe Blow's life.

Outside the Matrix, Neo is just an ordinary, physically atrophied human being; inside the Matrix he is "The One." Can the Matrix filmmakers possibly be saying that here's as good a place as any to make a divine connection?

Mythic personages abound in this cyberspace (as indeed the arrival of godhead is a shocking revelation in Gibson's beautiful first novel *Neuromancer*, followed by voodoo divinities in *Count Zero*). "The One" is a new Adam, a messiah . . . a superhero. He's come to show the way to the last human city, Zion. His "John the Baptist" is named after the Greek mythological divinity Morpheus, or "Sleep," the gatekeeper to dreams. There's also the femme fatale with the loaded name, Trinity, who resurrects her murdered lover with a kiss. Their rebel ship is named *Nebuchadnezzar*.

But is the Matrix just a gamer's shot at being more than he can ever hope to be in the corporeal world? By virtue of its special properties as a space defined by rational coding, is it just that a gifted hacker savant is able to rewrite the rules; via some super gestalt, is it that he's able to control and shift its representations to his advantage? Or is there some deeper voodoo, some hyper sympathetic magic putting the dreamers in touch with a larger plan subtending existence?

Within the Matrix, Neo is taken by Morpheus to meet the Oracle. It's a wonderful bit and a disturbing one. This Oracle is seeing things atemporally. This isn't a bending or breaking of Newtonian rules; here we're going quantum and relativistic at once. What code/representation/metaphor explains this? We're spookily closer to the divine here than anywhere else in the story.

Perhaps some undisclosed part of the Matrix is modeling heaven, the levels of hell, angels, devils and gods. How closely can you model a reality before it begins to merge identities with the thing being modeled? Like entangled pairs in quantum physics. Instant teleportation of behaviors over any distance, because the subject photons share an identity.

We don't know that the Oracle has any corporeal existence; Morpheus tells Neo that this middle-aged matron is very old, that she's been with the resistance since the beginning. She tells Neo that he's got a good soul. We really aren't in Kansas for sure now.

The Oracle takes us outside what we structurally understand about the two apparent realities in the film. She's not operating in a normal spacetime continuum. Now things get really big.

Is this all just too far out? The directors, the Wachowski Brothers, are just having fun, right? I'm sure they are. But it's not too far out. It also makes me wonder if we're seeing just how far this could really go. How about this: Once in the Matrix, how is it you know that you've left? I mean, "Morpheus?" Really. Perhaps everybody is still dreaming. The plane the *Nebuchadnezzar* exists on, just another level of the Matrix. Why not? What is there to tell you that you aren't in just another dream reality subtended by yet a deeper reality? One turning around an entirely different axis? (This at least would give some latitude for the origins of the Oracle's prowess and vision). With "Sleep" as your guide, just where is the rooster crowing? Wake up, you're asleep.

In fact, I'm sure the filmmakers would rather enjoy it if you wondered about your own reality. "How much of this is illusion that I'm living?" In cyberspace, old, old questions and mystical pursuits suddenly take on a fresh coat of digital paint.

The Hindus have a multi-leveled, multiple reality structure that has at its base Vishnu the Dreamer. Our reality is Vishnu's dream; he's dreaming us. He also dreams himself much like you can appear in your own dreams. He can move atemporally and instantly over any distance in this dream.

The denizens of the world can dream of Vishnu, worship him, model him in their minds. The Dream can dream the Dreamer. Confusing?

The relation of cyberspace to our own corporeality provides a compelling metaphor: Forget about the linear pursuit of ultimates and hierarchies. Quit even looking for the center of things. Maybe reality is holographic in nature and every single little connection in the matrix of existence carries an image of the whole. Perhaps we cannot see the end of this vast rolling cosmos, but maybe we can see into ourselves and come to an understanding; look at the geometry of internal and nearby relationships and try and draw some conclusions about the way of the world(s).

We may never be really certain about finding an ultimate "bottom" or "top" in the hierarchies of existence. But I'm not sure that we can't, by such relativistic contemplations, seek something akin to wisdom about such things; pierce the multilayered veil as it were and if not know the bottom or top of things, know about the dimension of wonder and perceive into the nature of existence.

We are on the astounding verge of our own perceptions. A bright edge that meltingly folds forward into the dark, creating the frontier as we go. A new wave of dreamspace seems to await our waking brains. Perhaps it's mind itself, dreaming.

Vishnu must have rolled over in his sleep and hit "enter."

About the Authors

PAT CADIGAN, acclaimed by the *London Guardian* as "the Queen of Cyberpunk," is the author of four novels—*Mindplayers, Synners, Fools,* and *Tea from an Empty Cup*—and three short story collections: *Patterns, Home by the Sea,* and *Dirty Work.* Some of her short stories have also appeared in *Letters from Home,* alongside work by Karen Joy Fowler and Pat Murphy. She continues to publish short fiction, with recent stories in *New Worlds, Dark Terrors 3, Disco 2000,* and the Christmas 2001 issue of *Interzone.* She was an editor and writer for Hallmark Cards in Kansas City for ten years before embarking on her career as a fiction writer in 1987. Since that time her Hugo and Nebula Award–nominated short stories have appeared in such magazines as *Omni, The Magazine of Fantasy and Science Fiction,* and *Isaac Asimov's Science Fiction Magazine,* as well as numerous anthologies. She moved to England in 1996, and now lives in North London with her husband, Chris Fowler, and their cat, Calgary.

BRUCE STERLING, author, journalist, editor, and critic, has written eight science fiction novels and three short story collections. He edited the anthology *Mirrorshades,* the definitive anthology of the cyberpunk movement. He also wrote the non fiction book *The Hacker Crackdown: Law and Disorder on the Electronic Frontier* (1992) available electronically on the Internet. He has written regular columns on popular science and literary criticism for *The Magazine of Fantasy and Science Fiction, Interzone,* and *Science Fiction Eye.* He also writes a Web log and runs a Web site and Internet mailing list on the topic of environmental activism and postindustrial design. He lives in Austin, Texas, with his wife and two daughters.

STEPHEN BAXTER's science-fiction novels have been published in the United Kingdom, the U.S., and in many other countries including Germany, Japan, and France. His books have won several awards, including the Philip K. Dick Award, the John Campbell Memorial Award, the British Science Fiction Association Award, the Kurd Lasswitz Award (Germany), and the Seiun Award (Japan), and have been nominated for several others, including the Arthur C. Clarke Award, the Hugo Award and Locus Award. Over one hundred of his SF short stories have been published, several of which have won prizes. His most recent book is a full-length novel, *Evolution,* published by Gollancz in November 2002. His novel *Timelike Infinity* and short story "Pilot" are both under development for feature films. Baxter's TV and movie work also includes development work on the BBC's *Invasion: Earth* and the script for Episode 3 of *Space Island One,* broadcast on Sky One in January 1998. His novel *Voyage* was dramatized by Audio Movies for BBC Radio in 1999.

JOHN SHIRLEY is the author of many novels, collections of stories including *Black Butterflies* (winner of the Bram Stoker Award and chosen for the *Publishers Weekly* list of year's best books), *Demons, And the Angel with Television Eyes, Eclipse,* and *City Come A Walkin'.* He was coscreenwriter of *The Crow* and has written for television and film extensively. The authorized Web site is www.darkecho.com/johnshirley. He lives in the San Francisco Bay area.

DARREL ANDERSON, a digital-art pioneer, emerged from the underground comix scene to create one of the earliest and longest running art Web sites, braid.com. With members of the BRAID collective and PCA Graphics, he created the animated CGI climax of the 1995 film *Johnny Mnemonic.* The Science Fiction Channel Web site features forty-eight of his images, and he is profiled in *Fantasy Art of the New Millennium II* by Dick Jude. His artwork has received top honors in numerous international award competitions, including Pixar's call for images and MacWorld's Macintosh Masters competition. Anderson actually works either side of the screen, as both programmer and artist. One of his latest developments, GroBoto, is an interactive art tool intended to allow children to explore their creativity, and artists to further theirs. Anderson's work can be seen and sampled at: braid.com

PAUL DI FILIPPO just celebrated his twentieth year as a freelance writer by publishing four books in 2002. His story "Karuna, Inc." was nominated for a World Fantasy Award. In 1994 he won the British Science Fiction Award. His previous novels include *Ciphers* (1991), *Lost Pages* (1998), and *Joe's Liver* (2000). He lives in Providence, Rhode Island, with his mate of twenty-seven years, Deborah Newton, a cocker spaniel named Ginger, and two cats, Mab and Penny Century.

KATHLEEN ANN GOONAN's latest novel, *Light Music* (HarperCollins/Eos, May 2002), completes her Nanotech Quartet, and was received with excellent reviews. The first book of the quartet, *Queen City Jazz,* was a *New York Times*

Notable Book; the third, *Crescent City Rhapsody*, was a Nebula finalist. Her unique melding of literature, science fiction, and music has been noted in *Scientific American*, along with the work of Greg Bear and Neal Stephenson, as being seminal contributions to nanotech science fiction. She has published over twenty short stories in various venues, and her novels and short stories have been published in France, Germany, Italy, Spain, Poland, Russia, and the United Kingdom. Her Web page is www.goonan.com.

MIKE RESNICK is the author of more than forty science fiction novels, twelve collections, two screenplays, and over 140 short stories. He has also edited thirty anthologies. He has won four Hugos and a Nebula, plus major and minor awards in the U.S., France, Japan, Spain, Poland, and Croatia. His passions are science fiction, Africa, horse racing, and musical theater.

WALTER JON WILLIAMS is a screenwriter, the author of *The Praxis* and the cyberpunk classic *Hardwired,* and a fourth-degree black belt in Kenpo. He has also authored another fourteen science-fiction novels and one short-story collection, as well as the ongoing licensed series *Star Wars: The New Jedi Order*.

DEAN MOTTER, illustrator, designer, writer, and editor, is a city boy by nature, so it is no surprise that architecture and urban life often figures prominently in his work. His two critically acclaimed Vertigo Comics miniseries, *Terminal City* and *Terminal City: Aerial Graffiti*, were nominated for a number of comics industry Eisner and Kurtzman Awards in 1997 and 1998. Currently he continues to labor happily in the comic book mines, most recently with the highly acclaimed graphic novel, *Batman: Nine Lives,* and is writing and illustrating Image Comics' *Electropolis*—yet another return to yesterday's future. Motter is perhaps best known as the creator of the influential 1980s comic book sensation *Mister X.*

IAN WATSON graduated from Oxford University with a first class honors degree in English language and literature, completed a research degree in nineteenth-century English and French literature, then lectured in universities in Dar es Salaam and Tokyo and taught futures studies at Birmingham (UK) Art and Design Centre before becoming a full-time SF author in 1976. His first novel, *The Embedding* (1973), won joint second prize in the John W. Campbell Memorial Award and, in French translation, the Prix Apollo. His most recent novel, *Mockymen*, appeared in 2003 from Golden Gryphon Press, which published his ninth story collection, *The Great Escape*, in 2002 to considerable critical acclaim. His first book of poetry, *The Lexicographer's Love Song*, appeared from DNA Publications in 2001. From 1990 to 1991 he worked with Stanley Kubrick on story development for what became Steven Spielberg's *A.I. Artificial Intelligence*, for which he has screen credit for screen story. He lives in rural England with a black cat.

JOE HALDEMAN is best known for *The Forever War*, a novel that won the Hugo, Nebula, and Ditmar Awards, and is now considered a classic of science fiction. His latest novels are *The Coming* and *Guardian* (December 2002). He has won five Nebulas and four Hugo Awards. His twenty novels, three story collections, six anthologies, and one poetry collection have appeared in eighteen languages. Haldeman's mainstream novels *War Year* and *1968* are based on his experience as a combat engineer in the Central Highlands of Vietnam. He teaches writing at Massachusetts Institute of Technology one semester a year, is an avid amateur astronomer, paints watercolors, and plays the guitar. His Web site is home.earthlink.net/~haldeman.

DAVID BRIN's popular science-fiction novels have been translated into more than twenty languages, including *The New York Times* bestsellers that won Hugo, Nebula, and other awards. His 1989 ecological thriller, *Earth*, foreshadowed global warming, cyberwarfare, and the World Wide Web. A 1998 movie, starring Kevin Costner, was loosely adapted from his Campbell Award winner, *The Postman*. *Foundation's Triumph* brought a grand finale to Isaac Asimov's famed Foundation Universe. Brin's latest novel, *Kiln People* (2002), portrays a coming era when a simple advance in technology allows anyone to achieve the ancient dream of being in two places at once. Brin is also a noted scientist and speaker/consultant about trends in the near future. His nonfiction book, *The Transparent Society: Will Technology Make Us Choose Between Freedom and Privacy?*, deals with issues of openness, security and liberty in the new wired-age. It won the 2000 Obeler Freedom of Speech Award of the American Library Association and a prize from the McGannon Foundation for public service in communications.

ALAN DEAN FOSTER's work to date includes excursions into hard science fiction, fantasy, horror, detective, western, historical, and contemporary fiction. He has also written numerous nonfiction articles on film, science, and scuba diving, and has produced the novel versions of many films, including *Star Wars*, the first three *Alien* films, and *Alien Nation*. Other works include scripts for talking records, radio, computer games, and the story for the first *Star Trek* movie. His short fiction has appeared in all the major SF magazines as well as in original anthologies and several "Best of the Year" compendiums. Five collections of his short-form work have been published. Foster was born in New York City and was raised in Los Angeles. He currently lives in Prescott, Arizona.

KAREN HABER is the author of eight novels, including *Star Trek: Voyager—Bless the Beasts*, coauthor of *The Science of the X-Men*, and editor of the Hugo-nominated essay anthology celebrating J. R. R. Tolkien, *Meditations on Middle-earth*. Her short fiction has appeared in *Asimov's Science Fiction* magazine, *The Magazine of Fantasy and Science Fiction*, and many anthologies. She reviews art books for *LOCUS* magazine and profiles artists for various publications, including *Realms of Fantasy*.

JAMES PATRICK KELLY has had an eclectic writing career. He has written novels, short stories, essays, reviews, poetry, plays and planetarium shows. His books include *Strange but Not a Stranger* (2002), *Think Like a Dinosaur and Other Stories* (1997), *Wildlife* (1994), *Heroines* (1990*)*, *Look into the Sun* (1989), *Freedom Beach* (1986), and *Planet of Whispers* (1984). His fiction has been translated into fourteen languages. He has won the World Science Fiction Society's Hugo Award twice: in 1996, for his novelette, "Think Like a Dinosaur," and in 2000, for his novelette, "Ten to the Sixteenth to One." He writes a column on the internet for *Asimov's Science Fiction* magazine and his audio plays are a regular feature on Scifi.com's "Seeing Ear Theater." He is currently one of fourteen councilors appointed by the governor of New Hampshire to the State Council on the Arts. He also sits on the Board of Directors of the New England Foundation for the Arts.

KEVIN J. ANDERSON is the author of numerous bestselling and award-winning science-fiction novels. Recent titles include *Hidden Empire, Hopscotch, Captain Nemo*, a series of prequels to *Dune* written with Frank Herbert's son Brian, as well as *Star Wars* and *X-Files* novels. An avid hiker, he has climbed the fifty highest peaks in the Rocky Mountains, and prefers to write while out in the wilderness.

RICK BERRY is known for, among other things, being the first artist to embrace the digital realm when, in 1984, he created, digitally, the cover for

William Gibson's *Neuromancer*. Since then he has evolved a style combining traditional oil paint techniques with cyber-imaging. His work has been exhibited throughout the U.S. and he's won many awards from both the SF and digital communities. He's produced concept art for television and, with Darrel Anderson and Gene Bodio, created a 3D Computer Aided Design cyberspace climax for the 1995 movie *Johnny Mnemonic*. He also created the 3D CAD Human Design Disc, an anatomical software model published by Antic Software. He has taught at the University of Tennessee and Adams State University, and been the AI symposia lecturer at Tufts University in Boston. A book of his collaborative work with Phil Hale, *Double Memory: Art and Collaboration*, was published in 1993. He's currently working on a collection of digital images with Darrel Anderson in the collaboration known as Braid. His Web site is: www.braid.com.